Introduction

A few months after I arrived in Beijing, in the fall of 2007, I was invited to attend a concert at the National Theater. I was running late and hailed a taxi. When I opened the door and got into the car, an overwhelming odor of sour sweat hit me, so pungent it turned my stomach. I figured it must have been several days since the driver had last showered. When we stopped at the first red light, I was stunned when the driver, clearly uncomfortable, turned around to say, "Miss, open your window because it stinks in here. What perfume are you wearing? It's unbearable."

This striking level of candor so typical of the Chinese people fascinated me from the start. At the time, the impression I had of them could be summed up in four or five common characteristics: self-sacrificing, tireless, capable of overcoming any adversity, and often lacking in empathy. I knew that in recent years China's economy had taken off at an astounding pace, and that the country had been traumatized by foreign colonialism, the famines of the Great Leap Forward, and the atrocities committed under the Cultural Revolution. They were busily preparing for their great debut on the world stage with the 2008 Olympic Games, but at the same time their government censured the Internet, punished activists, and tolerated alarmingly high levels of corruption.

But, who were the Chinese? Were they really so self-sacrificing? Were they promiscuous? Were they interested in what was going on in the rest of the world?

Over the next three years, I observed China from dozens of different angles. I traveled to Xinjiang to cover the most violent ethnic uprisings to occur over the past several decades. I watched young people make themselves over into rock stars, and saw old people get down on their knees in front of courthouses; demanding justice after their homes had been demolished. I attended the Olympics in Beijing, charged with polemics and patriotic pride.

In this climate Weibo, the local equivalent of Twitter, was launched, revolutionizing the Web. The West was now interested in China, regardless of whether some catastrophe claiming thousands of lives had just occurred there or not. International correspondents talked about the yuan's fluctuations, techno festivals, scandalous levels of air pollution, and the repression of dissidents. I interviewed hundreds of people from all rungs of the socioeconomic ladder, who gave me the keys to better understanding where China was coming from, and where it was heading. I made some wonderful friendships, and witnessed repulsive injustices. Many stereotypes I had held before were shattered.

But space in the media outlets I was working for was limited. Too many fascinating stories never saw the light of day. I chose the ten personal stories that made the strongest impact on me, to unlock the country that is still such a mystery for so many Westerners. That is how *From the Dragon's Mouth* was born.

In the first chapter, *Rich Kids*, we go inside the world of the *fu er dai*, the second generation of millionaire Chinese. Tim and Xiao Chen are "daddy's boys" who zip through the streets of Beijing in their Ferrari. Their families, closely connected to the highest circles of government, have mapped out the road to success for them. They don't have regular jobs, instead spending their time investing their money. It was quite something to see them in their element at the most exclusive nightclubs in the capital, surrounded by the colorful personalities of their privileged social set.

In *Kidnapped by His Own Government* I speak with the lawyer and activist Jiang Tianyong, one of the very few civil rights experts in China. In February 2012, coinciding with the Arab Spring uprisings, he was detained and tortured for two months by agents of the Ministry of Security. The lawyer reveals in detail what goes through the mind of a dissident, the moment he decided to cross the line, and why he would rather risk his life instead of retiring comfortably at a state-owned company.

For the protagonist of Chapter Three, *A Gay Husband Is Better Than None*, sex had always been taboo. Xiao Qiong is a *tongqi*, or "wife of a homosexual." Three years earlier she married her best friend, a gay man who wanted to put an end to his family's relentless pressure to settle down. It is estimated there are around sixteen million women like her in China, but most are too ashamed to admit to their situation. They only talk about it openly among themselves and on the Internet, using pseudonyms.

Silence: The Master Speaks tells the story of Du, an old man and highly respected kung-fu master, who at seventy is still as agile as an adolescent athlete. He can barely read and write, but he is the most sought-after master at martial arts tournaments. His disciples swat away mosquitoes around him and bow down in reverence. Master Du's biggest worry is not how he will survive on his meager pension, but the fact that there are fewer and fewer parks in Beijing where he can train.

In *Plunging into the Sea of Business: China's Entrepreneurs* we meet Yang Lu, a businesswoman and daughter of Communist Party military officers who makes a fortune giving courses in executive leadership. She teaches them about wine, how to talk about golf, and to keep their personal and professional lives separate, among other things. In a country where most companies are private but the State still controls the lion's share of the economy, it is not always easy to "plunge into the sea," the Chinese expression that describes venturing into the vast, uncharted waters of the business world.

Living Underground explores the polar opposite universe. Chen Erfei is one of three hundred million peasants from the countryside who have migrated to Chinese cities in search of a better life. He works as a security guard at an upscale residential development and sleeps in one of the underground bomb shelters that Mao Zedong had constructed in the sixties for fear of a Soviet attack, which have been converted into living quarters. Chen Erfei and others like him are the real heroes of China's economic miracle, keeping the country afloat even though they are ascribed second-class citizen status.

Twenty-four years old and unemployed, Ma Chencheng lives attached to the Internet. She perfectly represents *China 2.0*, the consumerist, apolitical youth whose tastes change at lightning speed. She never reads the official news outlets, preferring blogs instead. Ma showed me to what point the Web allows millions of people to express themselves, and how the Government counterattacks.

In *A Prostitute in Secret*, Mrs. Zhen's husband believes she works as a shop clerk. But for years, she has been meeting clients at an apartment owned by a wealthy businessman, with whom she maintains a special relationship. At one of our dinners (she makes an amazing spinach dish), she revealed to me what she has really been doing to pay for her son's education. She is always on a diet, because if she ever got fat she would have to lower her rates.

From his taxi, Zhang Xiaodong has seen the colossal transformation of China's urban landscape. He tells us all about it in *Beijing, Seen from a Taxi*. When he first began driving, he had to deal with tangled hordes of bicyclists. Now he spends three hours a day stuck in traffic jams. Like many others nostalgic for Maoism, he dreams of traveling to North Korea, to relive the China of the sixties.

The Dark Side of China introduces us to Linda, a brilliant, sharp-eyed journalist who saw the darkest side of her country when she went to work for a foreign television network. She doesn't always agree with her bosses' vision, but some Chinese still accuse her of being a traitor for working for "the enemy." For years, she has lived in the uncomfortable position of feeling obligated to defend her country to foreigners, and to criticize it to her compatriots.

This book is not a treatise on history or economics; it is a portrait of ten citizens of a country that could become the biggest superpower on the planet. They talk about their relationship with family, with power, and with the rest of the world. They tell us about what moves them, and how they make decisions; why they live in a dictatorship, and yet how they are so anarchic.

It was not easy to gain their trust; some had never spoken to a foreigner before. The key was to interview them myself in Mandarin, because most refused to allow another Chinese person to hear their stories, either out of fear or embarrassment. After months of conversation, long walks and one instance of police persecution, they all talked to me openly about their goals, dreams and frustrations. Where necessary I have used fictional names in order to protect them.

FROM THE DRAGON'S MOUTH

1

✦✦✦✦✦

Rich Kids

"Hand."

"Sorry, what did you say?"

"Hand," the man at the door repeats in a monotone. His coworker, another six-foot tall giant in charge of searching people's bags, motions to me that I have to hold out my hand to be stamped before going inside. The girls at the coat-check laugh, covering their mouths. The disco has increased its security measures: there are more customers with money than before, more drugs, more fights.

It's one of the "it" places in Beijing, built to an oversized scale, a minimalist's nightmare with bathrooms outfitted in black marble, walls covered in shiny black fabric, purple silk curtains, and large vases filled with artificial flowers. There is a baroque-style fountain next to the DJ booth, complete with a cherub. To fully appreciate the details, first the eyes have to adjust to the gloom. The discos in China are much louder and darker than in the West.

I'm looking for Xiao Chen. We have agreed to meet in the bar so we won't miss each other. I sit down on a barstool, as the couple next to me orders eight shots. The young woman brushes a lock of hair away from her face, takes one small glass in each hand, and squeals happily. Her companion holds her purse, as Chinese boyfriends typically do. He laughs and picks up a glass. They each down four shots one right after the other, and order another round.

The dance floor is deserted. Waiters rush around, serving the tables in the back, carrying buckets of ice, bottles, and trays of fresh fruit. The night has begun, and no one dances: now it's time for the *jiu ling* (酒令), the drinking games. They play with dice, cards, they play guessing games, or hand games. Some of them are ancient, dating back to imperial times, others are such recent inventions they incorporate the popular slang of the moment. They all serve the same purpose: to get the players drunk.

Someone gestures to me from a dark corner. I recognize Xiao Chen. He wears his short hair fashionably styled, rising in a little peak in the front. I go over and he shyly shakes my hand. "Welcome. Please, sit down."

Two petite young women look up at me and say hi. "This is Mimi, my girlfriend, and Li Lei, Tim's girlfriend. He's getting more drinks, he'll be right back," Xiao Chen explains, as he moves the girls' bags to clear a spot for me to sit. I sink down into the black leather sofa and apologize for being late, although I'm not. The Chinese generally like to get to appointments early. "Don't worry, we haven't even started playing yet," Li Lei says, winking at her friend. Mimi reaches into her Marc Jacobs bag and pulls out a set of dice.

"What do you like to play?" Mimi asks me, lighting up a pink cigarette. She offers me the pack, with stars and hearts on it. "Take as many as you want. They're imported from Japan."

Tim comes over with an ice bucket filled with beers, and dries his hands before shaking mine. "I see everything's all set for the dice game. Whenever you want. I'm going to destroy all of you," he says with a laugh.

Li Lei suddenly sits up straight, gathers her hair into a bun and takes off her limited edition Cartier watch, as attentive as a surgeon about to begin an operation. Mimi throws the dice.

The Chinese are generally very good at making calculations. Just playing games makes this very clear. They love to compete, make bets, and make a scene. After three rounds, Li Lei seems to be the winner. Not one strand of hair is out of place. Xiao Chen is flush from the alcohol, and has unfastened two of his shirt buttons. He calls the waiter over and asks for vodka and more watermelon. He buys two bottles; each one costs one hundred thirty dollars.

Mimi's agitated, she can't sit still. Her clinking bracelets are bothering her so she takes them off. She taps her fingers on the glass tabletop as she waits for her turn. Xiao Chen looks at her and laughs. "She's so competitive," he jokes, "if she doesn't win she won't be able to fall asleep later."

"Idiot," she retorts, and gives him a swat. "You're so useless." He rushes to give her a hug, but she pushes him away, offended. Then she relents and lets him put his arm around her.

A waiter who looks like a young teenager, with a downy moustache, takes our bucket away to refill it with ice. Our table costs 2,000 yuan, roughly 300 dollars, almost double what the waiter must make in a month working all night long, six nights a week. There is no tipping in China. The wait staff has to put up with just about anything, especially from customers at the tables.

Mimi stands up, a bit wobbly from all the drinks, and says she's going to the ladies' room. Li Lei grabs her bag and goes with her. They have to wait in line for a few minutes, so they use the time to update their Weibo accounts, the Chinese equivalent of Twitter. "Smile!" says Li Lei, and aims her iPhone at Mimi. She holds up her hand and makes a peace sign, and throws a kiss at the camera. Her friend laughs and quickly types out a message on her phone with her dark blue nails, painted to match her outfit.

The women's bathroom offers a stark lesson in class differences in China. The customers, like Mimi and Li Lei, are tall, with long, thick hair and perfect teeth. They protect their skin from the sun, and use special creams to maintain as white a complexion as possible. Adding up the cost of their clothes, makeup, jewelry and accessories, they are wearing thousands of yuan. They carry the very latest models of cell phones, and are not embarrassed about purchasing condoms from the disco's vending machine, preparing for what might transpire later. In contrast, the *ayi*, the women who work as bathroom attendants, stand several inches shorter, with olive complexions, and rough hands, discolored from bleach. They wear synthetic maroon uniforms, canvas shoes; their hair gathered in buns and covered by hair nets.

Every time a customer leaves a stall, the *ayi* go in to clean up after them. They carry huge wooden tongs to pick up any stray toilet paper that has landed on the floor. Mimi and Li Lei spend twenty minutes reapplying their makeup and fixing their hair. Transfixed, the *ayi* watch them as if they were movie stars, offering them paper towels to dry their hands. One of the *ayi* offers Mimi a devoted smile through the mirror. She has a pretty face, but her teeth are in terrible shape. Mimi doesn't notice the young woman looking at her. She puts on some lip-gloss and winks at me.

"Shall we go back to the table?" she asks, adjusting her bangs again.

The dance floor is packed now. The DJ is wearing a wool cap, even though the heat is stifling, and flirts with the girls lined up to talk to him.

"God, he's so hot!" a girl shrieks, and takes off her shoes to climb up onto the platform. She's about four feet tall without heels. Once she's up, she quickly puts on her high heels again and starts gyrating like a professional stripper. "Wow!" I say to her friend. "She sure can dance!"

"We all take pole dancing classes," she replies casually.

In Beijing, striptease and pole dancing classes are very popular. Women learn to take off their clothes and contort themselves like gymnasts to the rhythm of a Shakira song, one of their Western idols. The dance schools promise they will be back in shape just two months after giving birth, and the classes will heighten their sex appeal. "These dances put the spark back into relationships," said one instructor in an interview for a Beijing women's magazine. "Pilates won't do that."

Tim and Xiao Chen have already polished off the first bottle and get right to work on the second. Tim looks unaffected, his gelled hair and retro black-framed glasses still in place, but Xiao Chen is bathed in sweat and reeling. When he stands up to let us get past him, he stumbles and spills a drink.

"It's always the same," Mimi complains. "You can't drink."

Xiao Chen looks at her, glassy-eyed, raises his hands theatrically and croons a few lines from *Fairytale* (童话, *tong hua*), a romantic hit at the karaoke bars:

"*You have to believe, believe in us . . .*" he sings in falsetto.

Mimi grabs her bag and leaves in a huff. For a moment we're all speechless. Li Lei motions to Tim, and he gathers up Xiao Chen's things. "I think we have to leave. I'm sorry," Tim apologizes, "our friend Mimi is quite a character."

Embarrassed, Xiao Chen struggles to rebutton his shirt and shakes my hand. "We'll see you again soon," he slurs. "Good night," says Li Lei, and offers me her childlike hand. Then she repeats "good night" in English.

The young waiter moves some chairs aside so we can pass by.

5

Seeing there is still over a hundred dollars' worth of alcohol left, he sighs and starts emptying the ashtrays.

Tim, Xiao Chen and their girlfriends are what is known in China as *fu er dai* (富二代), children of the newly wealthy, widely considered spoiled and indulged. They live in a comfortable bubble, thanks to their parents' fortunes. They are unaware of how jam-packed and claustrophobic the Beijing metro is in the mornings: they get up whenever they please, and organize their day on their iPads, making plans to meet in restaurants, galleries and cafes. They do not have to worry about finding jobs or saving up to buy a house, like the rest of their peers. From one day to the next they plan pleasure cruises on yachts that cost tens of thousands of yuan. When they are asked what they do, they answer vaguely, "I'm in business."

Chinese millionaires are an evasive breed who generally try to avoid explaining exactly where their fortunes come from. What is clear is that their numbers are rising. According to the magazine *Hurun*, the Chinese equivalent of *Forbes*, in the middle of 2011, 960,000 residents of China had a net worth of over 1.5 million dollars. On average they are younger than forty, and most have made their money in private industry. Twenty percent made their fortunes in the real estate boom, while another fifteen percent had invested in the stock market. One thing they all have in common is their high-level contacts in government. In fact, three of every ten hold a political post themselves. During Mao's reign, the rich were seen as "capitalist exploiters" who should be persecuted, but in the eighties the Chinese government removed the stigma. Many analysts believe one thing the Communist Party has gotten right was to let the "capitalists" join their ranks, instead of making them feel marginalized from a political system whose legitimacy they could call into question.

In China, the wealthy generally fall into two categories: those who show off their money, and those who don't. People in the first group run red lights in their expensive luxury cars, are rude to waiters in restaurants, and spend outlandish amounts in the most exclusive shops. It's worth a trip to a high-end shopping center to see them in action, picking out designer handbags, fur coats and diamonds. They pay in cash, handing over huge wads of bills, since the highest denomination in Chinese currency is 100 yuan, or roughly fifteen dollars. They often travel abroad, visiting Paris, New York, London and Milan to see the latest trends and lighten their bank accounts: in 2011, according to China's Tourism Academy, over 70 million trips were made, a 25% increase over the previous year, and 68 billion dollars were spent on those trips. Western brands cost much more to consumers within China because of the taxes on imports, so when they visit other countries, Chinese tourists buy as much as they can (there is generally a limit to how much a single customer can purchase). The best foreign companies hire Mandarin-speaking staff to attend to their Chinese customers and offer them special products, like jade jewelry, or items featuring the animals of Chinese astrology.

The upper class in Beijing lives in private gated communities on the outskirts of the city, like most foreigners do. Touring these exclusive neighborhoods is quite an experience, beginning with the names: Versailles, River Garden, Champagne Town. . . . They always have a foreign name, but one that includes a very familiar word, like *paradise* or *château*. Once inside the security gates, there are broad avenues with fountains, colonnades and false stucco. The homes, complete with gardens, private swimming pools, and saunas, can sell for over six million dollars.

But the serious multimillionaires try to keep a low profile. They know they are in the spotlight, and if they attract too much attention, the government will audit their accounts. And in a country with such wide income disparity, where 60% of the gross domestic product rests in the hands of 0.03% of the population, people bristle at the sight of the rich enjoying their spoils. To minimize the risk of attacks and kidnappings, more and more of the wealthy are hiring bodyguards to protect them.

Tim and Xiao Chen were taught to be discreet. For example, Xiao Chen volunteers at a nongovernmental organization (NGO). His fellow volunteers could tell he was different from them, because he didn't have a paying job at all. Their suspicions were confirmed when they caught him behind the wheel of his BMW, which he always parked far away from the office.

When I first met Xiao Chen in the fall of 2010, the Internet was buzzing with discussions about children of the rich and the privileged treatment they received, because of the Li Gang case. One day, a high-ranking police officer in Hebei, the province surrounding Beijing, got a call informing him that his son, twenty-one-year-old Li Qiming, had run over two girls with his car. According to witnesses, he had been speeding around the university campus when he hit the girls who had been roller skating and drove off without stopping. One of the girls died, and the other was seriously injured. When some security guards blocked his path and ordered him to get out of the car, the young man, who had obviously been drinking, started shouting, "Go ahead, charge me! My father is Li Gang!"

Within hours, the incident was being heatedly discussed in chat rooms and forums all over the Internet, inspiring some outrageous parodies. Four days later, a Web page sprang up announcing a classic poetry contest, with only one requirement: the poem had to include the line "My father is Li Gang". Over six thousand people submitted poems. No matter how many times Li Gang appeared on state television, his eyes welling with tears, pleading for forgiveness on his son's behalf, Li Qiming became the poster boy for the flagrant abuses of the rich. It was one of the most widely covered stories in the news for 2010. In January 2011, the young man was sentenced to six years in prison, and had to pay the families of the victims a fine of $82,800.

Xiao Chen did not want to be seen as another spoiled rich kid with no scruples. The first time we met, he invited me to an Italian café patronized by the upper class (generally no one else drinks coffee), although not necessarily millionaires. We chatted a little about everything: his love of sports, how horrible the traffic jams were in Beijing, how great the coffee was at that café. . . . Once the small talk had run its course, he grew serious, and staring at his bottle of San Pellegrino, he said emphatically, "I want you to know I don't consider myself a daddy's boy."

"How would you describe yourself?" I asked, as delicately as I could manage in Chinese.

"I'm just a normal person. I have money, but I'm just like everyone else."

"But you don't have the same problems as most people your age, like not being able to buy an apartment, right?" I pressed.

Xiao Chen knew what I was talking about, and frowned, uncomfortable. Most Chinese hate it when the rich insist they are just like everyone else, but to him it didn't seem fair to generalize. "People curse us because they think to get to where we are, we must have had to step over everyone else, or committed some breach of ethics. But there are very few who hurt others. Most of the rich are good people. They have gotten a better education, and because of that, they wouldn't think of acting without first considering how others would be affected," he said in a rush, his voice trembling. I decided it would be best to change the subject.

We got together several times after that, but never alone. Xiao Chen went everywhere with Tim, his friend who was at the disco. Tim had studied in Canada, spoke fluent English, and had an answer for everything. Xiao Chen laughed at his friend's witty observations, drinking everything put in front of him until his shyness fell away and he could join in the conversation.

Watching them, it was hard to believe they had only known each other for five years. "Xiao Chen is like my little brother," Tim said the first day we were introduced. "We should have met much earlier, since we like all of the same things. Now we spend all day together to make up for lost time," Xiao Chen added with a laugh.

Once they were more comfortable talking to me, they explained that they got along so well because their backgrounds were so similar. Xiao Chen's parents were officials in the Army who made the switch to successful careers in business, jumping on the train in the eighties when thousands of state-owned companies were privatized. For Xiao Chen, that had meant being raised by nannies and chauffeurs. "My parents were gone all day working, so I had a pretty sad childhood. It was hard for me to make friends, because every two or three years I moved to a new school. I've lived in Henan, Tianjing, Nanjing and Harbin.[1] I keep in touch with five or six good friends, at the most, and they all live in a different city."

For a while he wanted to go abroad to study, like other young people of his social class, but his parents had other plans for him. "My mother didn't think I was mature enough to go abroad by myself, and she insisted I stay in China. I never understood why she wanted to keep me close by since she had barely taken care of me as a child, but she was adamant that we maintain contacts with the Army, and I was enrolled in a military boarding school."

Xiao Chen had thought that living with a group of his peers didn't sound so bad, compared with playing by himself. He spent six years in one of the most elite academies in China, rising every day at dawn, performing drills and exercises to the point of exhaustion. "I have very happy memories of that time," he told me. "There's a very special atmosphere in the military schools. You have hardly any freedom, everything has to be authorized, so in that sense the routine is boring. But you form incredibly close bonds with your classmates. They're like brothers, or even more than brothers. And I'm thankful to my parents for sending me there."

The school was coed, and Xiao Chen soon noticed Mimi, a girl in his class. She was sensible, and a talented long-distance runner. They became friends, and started dating in secret: romantic relationships among students were not allowed. Years later in 2007, once they were a well-established couple, they met Tim at a party for alumni of their academy and another boarding school. Tim had just gotten back from Canada, and had gone to the party to catch up with some childhood friends. Ever since, barely a day has gone by that they haven't seen each other.

Tim had not had much of a choice in the direction his life would take either. His parents were also business impresarios. They had always lived in Beijing, but were constantly traveling for work. When Tim was small they had left him with his grandparents and talked to him on the phone, almost always calling from an airport's VIP lounge just before boarding. Tim talks about them respectfully, but when he mentions his grandfather, who had turned a hundred a few months earlier, his face lights up.

"He's the one who raised me. He always tells me stories about the war, since he fought the Japanese in Harbin in the thirties. He's the most important person in my life."

When he was just eight years old, Tim was sent to a boarding school. "My parents didn't have time to take care of me. They wanted me to develop a strong personality, able to make sacrifices, and to get along in a group. If I had stayed at home, I would have spent most of my time by myself, and I wouldn't have developed the social skills I have now," he explains earnestly.

When Tim would go home for school vacations, his parents bought him whatever he wanted: computers, toys, racing bicycles. His friends were treated the same way, so it seemed normal. When he graduated, his parents informed him he would go to Canada to study finance. The plan was for him to return to China bilingual, with a foreign diploma under his belt. Tim had balked. "At first, I wasn't interested in that field of study. I would have rather studied graphic design. But they convinced me when they said I could go skiing every day in Canada. It was true: it's a paradise of snow!"

He spent seven years there which he describes as "glorious," using his father's credit card as much as he liked. He got his driver's license and bought a motorcycle and two cars. He and his friends went skiing at the best ski resorts in North America. He learned to speak English very well, and could have stayed there for work, but as soon as he graduated his family told him to come home.

"You never thought about disobeying them?" I asked.

He solemnly shook his head. "My father knew there were a lot of opportunities in China, and that I could be more successful here than abroad. That's why he asked me to come back. I don't feel like they pressured me. Our concept of family love is different than in the West; I learned that from my friends in Canada. We Chinese can be stubborn with our parents, but in the end we do what they say. We have a proverb that says, *listen to your elders, and you will earn your bread*."

Generous and vivacious, Tim loves surprises. One day he sent me a text message: "We want to invite you to dinner. I hope you can handle spicy food!" He gave an address, in the northeast of the city, and the room number 208A. I assumed it would be a hotel or club. When they want to celebrate something, the Chinese generally like to reserve a private room.

It turned out to be one of the best Korean restaurants in the city. When I arrived, there was a line of high-end luxury cars parked out front, most with dark tinted glass windows: three Audis, two Mercedes, one Ferrari, and two BMWs. The host who greeted customers at the door wore a headset, like a television host. The restaurant was an enormous glass cube, with three levels. There were large vases filled with orchids at the entrance, and a string quartet playing Mozart, right next to an indoor pond stocked with red carp. All wearing *hanbok*, the traditional Korean dress, the waitresses formed two lines to greet guests. "Welcome," they said in unison, first in Mandarin, and then in Korean, each time a customer walked through. The waiters, all with headsets, guided each diner to their table. Room 208A was on the second floor, just behind a traditional garden with rocks and real trees.

Tim, Mimi, Li Lei and Xiao Chen were already seated around the table. Tim had taken charge of ordering for everyone, in the typically generous Chinese style. The array of dishes looked like a wedding banquet: Spicy pickled cabbage, salads, three different kinds of Korean rice, shrimp, octopus and scallion pancakes, mushroom dumplings, and cold noodles.

"Come in and sit down! In one more minute we would have eaten everything!" joked Li Lei, gesturing with her chopsticks. Mimi smiled, chewing. She had curled her hair, and was wearing a beige dress with a rounded collar that made her resemble an antique doll.

A waitress served us porcelain bowls filled with blackened chicken and ginger soup, excellent for curing the common cold. Later she placed a hot stone in the center of the table and set down two trays with very thinly sliced veal. "Xiao Chen will be in charge of the barbeque," Mimi announced. Obedient, Xiao Chen picked up the tongs and began marinating the filets in sauce before placing them on the hot stone.

Li Lei picked at her salad, had some soup and said she was full.

She lit a pink cigarette. Tim and Xiao Chen also smoked, but they preferred Chunghwa tobacco, favored by business magnates. It's the brand handed out at official banquets, the most patriotic cigarette because the box is red with five yellow stars, just like the Chinese flag, and features a picture of Tiananmen Square. The cigarettes are supposed to taste like plums.

It was clear that the four friends got along very well. They started telling stories about people they all knew from boarding school. With a flare for the dramatic, Tim had to stand up to act out his stories. The rest laughed and laughed, Li Lei had tears streaming down her cheeks. Xiao Chen looked up at his friend admiringly while finishing off a bottle of *soju*, Korean rice liquor. "These two met in boarding school," Tim said, gesturing to Xiao Chen and Mimi. "Ask her how she got in, because it's a mystery."

Everyone chuckled. I looked at Xiao Chen, but it was Mimi who spoke up. "It's a very long story, so don't ask for details," she joked. "Basically, my parents are not in the military, but I got into the academy because they had some good contacts." She picked up a piece of cucumber with her chopsticks and took a small bite. "You know," she said pointedly, "in China, contacts are very important."

She was referring to *guanxi*, (关系), which loosely translates to "network of contacts," but to the Chinese it means so much more. It is a key that opens doors to attending a good school, getting free concert tickets, or getting out of paying a traffic ticket. Taken to extremes, it can get a business awarded a public contract worth millions, or keep a criminal from going to jail.

"Did you want to go into the military?" I asked Mimi.

"Military? Me?" she replied, puzzled. "How boring! It's just that in China, people in the military have a special status. Going to their schools is the way to land a good job."

It was something else these four friends had in common: their parents had set everything up so they would be part of the elite. "They have given everything to us," Xiao Chen explains. "They have made things very easy, but that also brings a lot of pressure with it." Tim nodded. "All parents want their children to be successful in life," Xiao Chen went on, "but we have been groomed for it since we were children. We can't disappoint them."

Almost half of the millionaires in China want to leave the country, according to a study published in October 2011 by the magazine *Hurun* and the Bank of China. They want their children to get an education abroad, and to get away from environmental contamination. They also want to flee judicial insecurity: they know they could fall into disgrace overnight, as has happened with dozens of business magnates and some especially well-off government officials.[2] One of the best examples of this is Huang Guangyu, president of the electronics and home appliance retail chain Gome. In 2007, the media described him as the quintessential entrepreneur, entirely self-made, who had started off selling radios in the street, and managed to build up the greatest fortune in China. He appeared on the list of millionaires published in *Hurun*, and three years later was sentenced to fourteen years in prison for illegal business practices, insider trading and corporate bribery.

To avoid meeting the same fate, the rich try and avoid appearing on any public lists. Many emigrate as soon as they can. The most popular destination is the United States, followed by Canada and Singapore. They apply for a foreign investor visa, which guarantees they will eventually be eligible for permanent residency. Every year, the United States grants ten thousand visas to foreign investors who put a million dollars into a local business, or half of that amount if it's in a rural or high-unemployment area. In 2007, two hundred and seventy Chinese millionaires applied for this type of visa.[3] Three years later, there were almost three thousand applicants. Not all of their applications were approved, because certain requirements have to be met,[4] but most are willing to pay thousands of dollars to various agencies to help them with the paperwork.

Tim's family is an exception. They are deeply nationalist, and have never considered leaving their country. When Tim was studying in Vancouver, his fellow Chinese students, all from very wealthy families, dreamed of one day becoming Canadian citizens. They wanted to buy their homes there, where they could really own them. In China, one can own a car, a business, or a yacht, but legally the ground on which a home is built belongs to the State.[5] In spite of everything, Tim's parents wanted him to come back: they had some good contacts in Beijing they didn't want to go to waste.

When he first got back to China, Tim felt strange. He had been abroad for seven years, and couldn't pick up on social cues. His father subjected him to intensive training, taking him out every night to meetings and parties. He wanted him to watch and listen very carefully, and then choose what type of business he wanted to launch. Money was no object. "My father's friends explained to me the rules of being a business owner in China," Tim said. "The first is to be a good, honest, humble person. Listen to the advice of others to try and compensate for your own weaknesses. And it's very important to be well-spoken and eloquent, because most deals are closed thanks to personal relationships."

He emphasized that in China, first you make friends, and then you get down to business. "In America, it's possible for two associates to not have anything in common outside of the business. Here, it's just the opposite. Sometimes that can be a problem, because if a friend makes you a business proposition, even if it's not very promising, you have to accept it, because he's your friend."

16

Tim decided to start up a company to promote Chinese culture. His family did not pressure him to see any gains in the short term. The most important thing was that the project had a certain glamour factor, and that it related to China. "Living abroad, I realized that each country has its own distinct flavor. But a lot of young people here seem to reject their own culture. They prefer imported trends, Facebook, hip hop. Western styles are becoming more prevalent, while Chinese idiosyncrasies are being drowned out. If we keep going on like this, within two hundred years our country will be just like any other. We have to make the most of who we are."

The model to follow would be Japan, which has succeeded in making their thousand-year-old traditions chic, exporting them to the rest of the world. "I'm sure you've heard of the Japanese tea ceremony, and their tradition of arranging flowers. They both originated in China," Tim pointed out. "In ancient times, preparing tea, burning incense, learning the arts of floral arrangement and calligraphy were the main sources of entertainment for the Chinese upper class. During the Tang dynasty, a monk named Jianzhen[6] introduced these practices to Japan. The Japanese infused them with ceremonial ritual, and then sold them as their own. And they make millions."

Now, Tim organizes parties for lovers of the traditional Chinese arts. "We expose them to purely Chinese culture," he explains. "We want people to at least know what is Chinese, and what has been imported from somewhere else." In the end, the events are for millionaires to mingle, make contacts and close deals.

I asked Tim if he considered himself a nationalist, and that seemed funny to him. "Are you asking if I like my country? Of course," he laughed. "Don't you like yours? But that doesn't have anything to do with my business. I started my company because my family suggested it, but also because of my knowledge of marketing and finance, I believe traditional Chinese culture has a great deal of potential. It's not the only thing I'm involved in, I'm also an investor in other companies. The culture business allows me to meet well-positioned people, it gives me access to other companies that I could invest in. Everything is connected, you see?"

Next to him, Mimi seemed bothered. She nervously touched her tear-shaped earrings, and interrupted Tim to ask abruptly, "But do you really believe the story that there's democracy in the West?" The table fell silent. Mimi didn't wait for an answer. "In the West," she went on, "they think democracy is some kind of religion. But those countries aren't perfect. Look what's happening with the crisis. Here in China, what matters to people is that they're living much better than they did before."

Li Lei, who works at CCTV, the main state television broadcaster of China, watched us as if we were guests on a televised debate. She was the most reserved of the group, and, according to Xiao Chen, the most brilliant. "What do you think of the Chinese government?" she asked, as she filled my glass with more liquor. I answered diplomatically, "It doesn't matter what I think. I'm here to learn what *you* think." Mimi's dour mood suddenly lifted. "You've said everything while saying nothing . . . it's like you're Chinese!" she giggled. "Let's not talk politics, it's so boring," Mimi said. "Did you know my mother wants to go to the museum of sex with me? She saw a report we did about it on television the other day, and she's called me three times already to ask me when I'm going to take her."

The waitresses came to the door and asked for permission to clear the table. They brought us two trays of fresh fruit and small green tea custards, compliments of the house. Tim proposed a toast to the new sports car he was going to pick up the following day. He didn't want to say exactly which model it was, since he wanted to surprise Li Lei. It was a luxury brand, because he had been on a waiting list for months. Xiao Chen told him he would take the day off to go along with him. "That's a true friend. But it's not like you have to work anyway, since your family gives you such a generous allowance," Tim joked.

Xiao Chen turned red. "I *do* work," he protested, looking at me. "My parents and I have several real estate companies, and we sell and invest in properties." He acknowledged that his hours were flexible, allowing him to spend time doing what he liked, skiing in the wintertime and playing golf in the summer. Tim had had personal instructors since he was a child, and he was teaching his friend. And they liked to travel. "We like to go to Hainan.[7] We hardly ever leave the country, because we would have to apply for a visa to go almost anywhere," Xiao Chen explained. "And I have to stay on top of my businesses, I can't travel very far."

I asked him if he liked the world of real estate. "Well . . . A business has to have two qualities: you have to like it, and it has to be profitable. If you turn something you like into a business, you can spend many years on it. If your sole objective is to make money, once you do, you'll start thinking about changing fields. In general, the Chinese run businesses for the short term, to make money."

"This is a very materialistic country," Mimi joked.

"But family is still important to us," Tim observed. "People still have a sense of family responsibility and duty. On the other hand, the competition is fierce. There are too many people, and everyone's trying to get ahead. When I got back, I couldn't get used to it." He opened up another bottle of *soju*.

Xiao Chen grew serious, perhaps because of the effect of the alcohol. "For me, the worst part is that people think badly of us because we have money. We need to be recognized too. For example, if we buy a house, people say our parents paid for it. That makes me uncomfortable, because maybe it's not like that. People don't know what they're talking about. I wish I didn't care what they thought of me, but I do. And that affects my dreams."

I asked them what their dreams were, and Mimi laughed. "I don't have any," she said. She was very drunk. "Life is so dark." They all laughed. Xiao Chen thought for a while before answering. "Mine is to live through a tornado. It must be brutal."

We were the last ones to leave the restaurant. The waiters were sweeping up, and they bowed respectfully and said goodbye as we walked out. Tim and Li Lei offered to drive me in their 4x4, but I wanted to walk for a while and get some air after drinking so much at dinner. Xiao Chen awkwardly held Mimi's arm, supporting her as she teetered atop her impossibly high heels. He helped her get into his Ferrari convertible.

"Good night, sleep well," Xiao Chen said, shaking my hand. Mimi smiled faintly as she leaned back in her seat. He started up the car, loudly revving the engine and then they were off, zooming past the skyscrapers and fading into the city. A little boy walking on the sidewalk with his grandfather burst into tears, startled by the sudden roar.

2

◆◆◆◆◆

Kidnapped by His Own Government

F our white walls, a bare light bulb hanging from the ceiling that was always on, twenty-four hours a day, and a battered mattress in the corner. Nothing else. Jiang Tianyong, a lawyer, spent two months in that room, for defending human rights in China. He had not committed any crime. He was just one of the few lawyers in the country who dared to openly question the system.[1] Like many other dissidents, he had been kidnapped by the police, interrogated and tortured, and held in a secret location in Beijing which he could not identify because they had covered his head when they brought him there.

That was in February, 2011. While Jiang Tianyong went through the worst experience of his life in the Chinese capital, thousands of miles away the Arab Spring uprisings had reached the boiling point. In Tunisia, the people had forced dictator Ben Ali to step down, and in Egypt, Hosni Mubarak had been pushed out after thirty years in power. The news seeped inside China, in spite of the censorship. The Government was on high alert. What if the same thing happened in China? Authorities feared a repeat of the Tiananmen Square protests of 1989, when hundreds or possibly thousands of protesters (there are no official numbers) had been killed by the army.

And the months leading up to the Arab uprisings had been especially tense for Beijing. In December 2010, the dissident writer Liu Xiaobo won the Nobel Peace Prize. Along with three hundred other Chinese intellectuals, professor, essayist and poet Liu Xiaobo had composed Charter 08, inspired by the Czech Charter 77, demanding greater freedoms and an end to the one-party system. Posted on the Internet, Charter 08 attracted thousands of signatures of support before disappearing from cyberspace. Liu Xiaobo also disappeared: on Christmas day, 2009 he was detained and later sentenced to eleven years in prison for "inciting subversion to State power," a classic sentence leveled against dissidents. When the West awarded him the Nobel, Beijing refused to allow him to leave prison to go accept the award. In December 2010, at the ceremony in Oslo, an empty seat was placed on stage in Liu's name. Outraged, the Chinese government asserted that the award was part of a "Western plot against China." The Government responded by ramping up diplomatic and trade pressure on Western countries, censuring activists even more, and further restricting access to the Internet. For example, the day before the award ceremony, the news Web sites of the BBC, CNN and the Norwegian state broadcaster NRK were blocked throughout mainland China.

That was the state of affairs when the Jasmine Uprisings began in the Arab world. Although events there barely reverberated in China,[2] the authorities were determined to squelch any sign of dissidence, to make sure it didn't get out of control. The Arab Spring coincided with the worst campaign of repression in China in two decades, and the lawyer Jiang Tianyong was one of its victims.

W ith shaggy hair, pants tied above his waist and wearing black plastic shoes, Jiang Tianyong looks more like a street vendor than a legal expert. In China, intellectuals often give interviews in their homes, and may open the door wearing a bathrobe and Winnie-the-Pooh slippers. They will pause an interview to loudly spit if they feel the need: they are humble, extremely cooperative and helpful, and what matters most to them is the essence of the conversation.

Jiang would have liked to talk to me in his own apartment, but it was not possible. He had been released from custody a few months earlier, and agents have been trailing him ever since. In order to be set free, among other things he had to promise the police that he would not have contact with any foreigners, much less journalists. The best thing is to meet at the office of the NGO where he serves as an advisor. He cannot work anywhere else since the government revoked his license to practice law. An hour before our meeting, he lets me know through a third party that the location has been changed. He's not sure we have been followed, but that's just how it goes for dissidents in China. They must always be on guard, just in case.

W hen we finally do meet, he gives me a firm handshake. He has a very warm smile, slightly stooped shoulders, and an informal, friendly demeanor. He jokes about the heat, and how ferocious the mosquitoes in Beijing can be. It feels like we have just gotten together to have a few beers, not to talk about the terror he lived through. But when he begins his story, he tells it flawlessly, remembering every detail, often pausing thoughtfully. I have interviewed other torture victims who were unable to string two sentences together, their gaze unfocused, panicked by everything that reminded them of their ordeal, whether it's a closed door, or a damp towel. Jiang sits calmly and listens, attentive. His hip still aches. While he was detained, the police made him spend several weeks in the same position, his back completely straight and his arms extended over his knees. Ever since, he has had intestinal problems, and the skin on his buttocks is hypersensitive because he developed painful sores from sitting motionless for so long.

The first thing we get straight is whether his real name will be in this book or not. "If by the time you're finished writing I'm allowed to talk to foreigners, then you can use it; but if not, use a pseudonym and change the names of all the cities and neighborhoods," he requests. Aside from this, when he tells me his story he holds nothing back. He talks about what had motivated him to be a legal defender of civil rights, one of the most dangerous professions in China, about how he came under increasing pressure, and what he was thinking the day the security forces of his own country kidnapped him.

C hinese activists are a very small, tight circle. They are not national heroes by any means. When Liu Xiaobo won the Nobel Prize, for example, the vast majority of Chinese citizens did not even know who he was. Among themselves, Chinese dissidents form a close-knit family, even though some members don't always get along, like real relatives. They know there is a red line (and that is what they call it) that the Government will not let them cross. They can talk about certain topics, like unfair rents and wide income disparity, or the exploitation of internal migrants in the cities. But they know if they dare to openly question the heart of the matter, the one-party system, their days of relative freedom are numbered.

Three days before they kidnapped him, Jiang went out to a restaurant on the west side of Beijing to meet with some other lawyers. Some luminaries in the fight for human rights were among the group, including Teng Biao and Tang Jitian. They had gotten together to decide how they could help their old friend Chen Guangcheng, a blind activist who criticized the forced sterilizations and abortions of thousands of women,[3] spent four years in prison, and was later placed under house arrest until his daring escape in April, 2012.[4] At their dinner meeting, the lawyers decided to go see Chen in his town in Shandong province, even though they knew it was likely they would be detained by authorities before reaching his house. During the period that Chen was under house arrest, many would-be visitors were attacked as they tried to approach his home.

Jiang's trip to visit his friend was over before it began. As he left the restaurant that night, a police officer was waiting for him. He escorted Jiang to a police station, where several agents shoved him around and barked questions at him. "They wanted to know why we had gotten together at the restaurant, and if it had anything to do with the Jasmine Uprising in the Arab world," he explains. "I assured them that had nothing to do with it, so they let me go."

Three days later, he got a phone call. It was an official from the State Security Bureau.[5] He remembers the conversation went like this:

"Mr. Jiang, we need to speak with you for a moment. Come outside, please."

"I'm not in my apartment. I came over to my brother's to have lunch."

"We know. We're here. Come down please."

As soon as he stepped out the front door onto the street, an agent grabbed his phone, while another put a jacket over his head, wrapping it so tightly over his face he could barely breathe. They shoved him into a van, and he lost consciousness.

Wwhen he came to, he was in the room with the white walls, his face resting against the floor. The damp concrete felt soothing against the bumps and bruises he had sustained. He did not have to check to make sure the door was locked. After the beating, he immediately understood that he had been taken to a "black jail". These illegal dungeons are not regular prisons; they are rooms the Chinese government maintains all over the country in the basements of state hotels, hospitals, asylums, or rental apartments. Beijing adamantly denies their existence, but even the very restrained official press makes reference to these black jails, used to hold political dissidents or so-called "petitioners," common citizens who have spoken up against state corruption or abuses of the system.

In theory, ever since imperial times, any Chinese citizen has had the right to protest against the illegal appropriation of their land, corruption, or abuses of national, regional and local authorities. All of the provincial capitals have an office dedicated to registering complaints. But, in practice, woe be it to anyone who dares to actually protest. It reflects badly on local authorities if high numbers of complaints are registered in their districts, because they will then have to offer an explanation to their superiors. Protesters are highly inconvenient, so orders are often issued for their arrest, before their complaints can even be officially filed. Some public functionaries and provincial police departments pay local thugs between twenty and forty dollars a day to seize protestors and bring them into secret custody, according to a chilling report from Human Rights Watch.[6]

The petitioners suffer all manner of abuse in the black jails. The least resistant are usually released as soon as they withdraw their complaints, but they often suffer from posttraumatic stress as a result of the beatings and threats. Activists like Jiang Tianyong are only released once they have been subjected to *xi nao* (洗脑), or "brain washing," like the old Maoist ideological reeducations. Finally, there are the detainees that make the authorities the most uncomfortable, because they have faced off directly against the Party or a state-run company. They are generally shipped off to forced-labor camps, where they can be held without trial for up to four years. In the very worst cases, they are held in *an kang* (安康), psychiatric hospitals administered by the Ministry of Security. According to some reports, this particular scenario most closely qualifies as a living hell: citizens who are perfectly sane are locked up with the seriously mentally ill, medicated by force, and could stay there until they die. That was the sad fate of Chen Miaocheng, an employee of the state petroleum giant Sinopec. In 1995, Chen was committed to a mental hospital against his will, suffering from "paranoid schizophrenia," according to his medical report. In December 1996, his doctors insisted that he should be released, but the hospital would not let him go without authorization from Sinopec. The petroleum company refused to grant it, and twelve years later, Chen died in the hospital. The autopsy report concluded that he had died from pneumonia. The legal battles waged by Chen's widow were in vain, and Sinopec emerged unscathed. From this perspective, Jiang Tianyong was lucky to have only been held and tortured, and not committed to a mental institution.

He barely remembers anything from his first night in captivity. They gave him such a beating his ears were ringing and the room was spinning. "I reached the point where I no longer felt any pain," Jiang explains. The worst came on the third day, when an agent from the Ministry of State Security came into the room:

"You're going to have to follow the rules from now on," he announced robotically. "Every morning at six o'clock you will get up, and the first thing you will do will be to say to me, 'Sir, forgive me. I am awake now. I love my country and I accept the education the

Government has prepared for me.' Is that clear? Your life is in our hands now, do you understand?"

Two people stood guard over him at all times, rotating in six-hour shifts. He was not allowed to talk, except to ask for water, or to go to the bathroom. The two guards accompanied him to the restroom.

"Can you sing?"

Jiang humbly replied that he didn't know how.

"Fine, then you will read aloud until we tell you to stop," the agent said, handing him a book of revolutionary songs.

Every morning he would have to read the lyrics to "Oh Party, My Dear Mother", "Wave the Red Flag with Five Stars"[7] and "Red Flag with Five Stars, You Are More Important Than My Own Life". Jiang said yes to everything, no matter how surreal the demands were. He knew from other dissidents what could happen to him if he resisted.

His captors had promised him he would be allowed to eat and sleep at certain hours, but they began to use those times to interrogate him instead. He went for several days without any sleep, while two agents from the State Security barked questions at him: Why had he defended members of Falun Gong,[8] why had he taken on the cases of peasants thrown off their lands, and what contacts did he have with foreigners. "I tried to tell them that my head was about to explode, that I needed to rest a little so I could remember, but they didn't care, they just kept at it until five o'clock in the morning. At six I had to get up and read the patriotic songs. Once they made me get off the chair and sit down on the floor, in such uncomfortable positions that my testicles became swollen. I could hardly urinate," Jiang recalls.

Nothing about his experience came as a surprise to him, since he had heard very similar stories from several colleagues about their detentions. "The worst part was being surrounded by white walls, with nothing to look at, and nothing to read. After a few days I felt dizzy all the time. I knew this was part of my reeducation, they want the prisoner to be disoriented," he says. He forced himself to keep his mind alert. He counted, forward and backward, backward and forward. He visualized laws, contracts, sentences. And he thought a great deal about the old road that went from his childhood home to the center of town, about what his life had been before he had landed in that room with the white walls.

How does one become a dissident? Jiang didn't grow up in an intellectual environment; his family were peasants steeped in Maoist propaganda. He had had a simple, rural childhood. They went to the bathroom in a ditch, which is common in the countryside, and he was often late to school because he played in the cornfields along the way. He was curious, bright and happy. Sometimes he forgot to do his homework. In other parts of the world, he would have been a mischievous boy with good potential, but spontaneity is penalized under the strict Chinese system, and only model students who always obey are successful.

Every month, the school posted a list ranking all the students, from first to last. It is a fundamental part of China's education system: making known to all which students got the worst grades, and their families. Jiang was always ranked among the last. His parents, their faces browned and wrinkled from working in the sun, pleaded with him to try harder so he could get out of the village one day. "You see how hard life is here for the people in Henan," they would tell him, "You have to do whatever you can to change your destiny, and go to university."

It was 1977, and the Cultural Revolution[9] had just ended, a period of real terror and xenophobia that left China mired in economic and intellectual misery. Mao had recently died, setting off an uncertain time of internal power struggles within the Communist Party. People who had been accused of being counterrevolutionaries began to be "rehabilitated." But in the countryside, where Jiang lived, the situation was still unchanged, and the peasants struggled just to have enough to eat. The government began to fear that the same disasters of the Great Leap Forward could be repeated, when more than twenty million people had died of starvation.[10]

Jiang was only seven years old, but what he saw going on around him was troubling. If his parents were poor as mice, why did they have to hand over part of their harvest to the local government? "I remember seeing them trudging down the mountain on a stiflingly hot day, carrying sacks of grain weighing a hundred thirty pounds down to the Party office. Three miles with those huge loads, and they were gritting their teeth, trying not to lose their footing," he remembers. One incident made a particularly strong impression:

"The people in our village gave away the best grain, clean and dry. But the Party chiefs always gave them a hard time, and insulted them. One day they said the grain wasn't good enough because it was damp. There was no convincing them otherwise. The peasants, including my parents, had to spread all the grain out on the cement, in front of the local government office. They spent all day drying it. When the sun started to set and they began to gather it all up, there was a sudden downpour. I will never forget the look of desperation on their faces as the grain got soaked."

The contradictions between the countryside and the cities grew more pronounced after 1978, when Prime Minister Deng Xiaoping took over the reins of power, and put into motion a series of economic reforms that opened the country up to the rest of the world. China and the United States reestablished diplomatic relations, and students and tourists began to arrive. In 1979, while Deng was on an official visit to the United States, he was shown on Chinese state television wearing a cowboy hat at a rodeo in Texas.

In the schools, teachers continued to act as mouthpieces for the Communist Party, but they talked about openness, protecting citizens, and the progress China was making. "Every day, in politics class, we recited many rules and regulations from memory. I knew them all, but I didn't understand what the purpose was," Jiang recalls. "For example, we chanted that the home of each person was protected by law, but after I would think about how in our time, party officials would go right into people's houses whenever they wanted. I began to see the dissonance between what they taught us and the reality."

The eighties had ushered in a certain intellectual renaissance in the wake of the Cultural Revolution, before the Tiananmen Square massacre at the decade's close. The government still exercised tight control, but many artists remember that some spaces of relative freedom and counterculture opened up, which were harshly criticized by conservatives. The most prominent example was a provocative documentary titled *Heshang* (河殇, "River Elegy"), which was broadcast by the official state television network CCTV in June, 1988. *Heshang* used the Yellow River as a metaphor for China, and tried to explain in six episodes why the country lagged behind the rest of the world. To the filmmakers, the most powerful symbols of their civilization which dated back millennia, the Great Wall or the Yellow River, were holding them back: the wall kept them isolated, and the riverbed was covered in mud, which slowed the current. The documentary supported the reforms which had been proposed by the Party's Secretary General Zhao Ziyang, but it deeply offended its most conservative wing.

The last episode of *Heshang* made a clear reference to the dictatorship, and defined democracy as transparent, reflecting the will of the people.[11] It had a profound impact on the public, who for the first time saw Confucianism and traditional Chinese ideologies called into question on television. A few months later, in the spring of 1989, Jiang began reading in the papers that thousands of students had gathered in Tiananmen Square in Beijing, just a few yards away from the national seat of the Government. Information surfaced slowly, but even the euphemisms employed by the official state propaganda machine made people think that something was brewing in the capital. Jiang and some friends started getting together in between classes to talk about the editorials in *The People's Daily*. "On April 26, I will never forget, the paper said the students were counterrevolutionaries, and talked about the protests as a planned insurrection," Jiang remembers. "Then we all knew this thing was really important."

In Beijing, an inflection point in modern Chinese history was gestating. Thousands of people had begun to question how the Government did things. And they were doing it in a place charged with symbolism: Tiananmen Square, in front of the Forbidden City, where emperors had lived, right near the seat of Government, and Mao's mausoleum.

The protests went on for seven weeks, with varying degrees of intensity. The beginning of the movement is often designated as April 15, coinciding with the death of ex-Secretary General of the Communist Party, Hu Yaobang. Two years before, he had broken with the party to support a student demonstration, a position which cost him his post in the Politburo. Some students believed he had been treated unfairly, and at his funeral demanded that his image be restored, gathering in the famous square.

Intellectuals and workers began to gather alongside the students, and gradually a diverse movement coalesced. Some demanded greater freedoms, and that political reforms be instituted along with the economic reforms, as had taken place in the Soviet Union; others protested against inflation, corruption, and social injustice. Some believed the government was focusing all of its efforts on modernizing the countryside, while neglecting the cities, where unemployment was on the rise.

The Communist Party responded through its official newspaper, *The People's Daily*. The editorial that Jiang and his classmates read together after class lambasted the protesting students in Beijing as being antirevolutionary, and fomenting chaos. This incensed the protestors, who considered themselves patriotic. They said they wanted to improve China, not betray it. Over the following weeks, students boycotted classes, and thousands went on hunger strikes.

This was the scene on May 15, 1989 when Mikhail Gorbachev landed in Beijing. In terms of diplomatic protocol, his official visit was a disaster: the Soviet leader could not even enter the Forbidden City, as over a million protesters, many carrying posters, were blocking the entrance to the ancient imperial palace. The students lauded Gorbachev for his increasingly open, progressive policies, and even delivered a letter to him. But to Chinese authorities, the episode was an embarrassment. Five days later, Beijing declared martial law.

Some members of the Politburo wanted to negotiate with the students, but hardliners won out, insisting that Tiananmen Square had to be cleared of all protesters no matter the cost. On the night of June 4, the Government issued the order for soldiers in tanks to take over the square. The tension had been simmering for weeks, and fearing the worst, many parents tried to keep their children from going. Witnesses of the attack remember gunshots, screams, panic and confusion, and blood running in the streets. The massacre did not take place in Tiananmen Square proper, but in the surrounding streets, turning the area into an inescapable trap. There were bodies in front of subway entrances, lying in gutters and at bus stops, according to mothers of some of the victims. How many were killed that day has never been determined, there may have been hundreds or as many as several thousand victims. Over the next days, many desperate families went around to hospitals and morgues, searching for loved ones. Eventually, several doctors admitted that they had been given explicit orders not to tend to the wounded, or to release bodies of the dead to their families under any circumstance. Thousands of people were detained and tortured, and many others were exiled. Foreign journalists were subject to more harassment than ever from authorities,[12] and some were forced to leave the country.[13]

Six hundred miles away, in his village in Henan, several months passed before Jiang found out about what had happened. He had only known that students and workers had been protesting in the square. "My friends and I didn't plan to go to Beijing, we didn't have money for the train ticket. We had to go by what was reported in the papers, but they hardly said anything. What got my attention was that, before June 4, many of our teachers supported the students in Tiananmen, but after that date, most of them reversed themselves." The subject was becoming taboo, until Jiang only had a few friends with whom he could talk freely about it. To this day, millions of Chinese do not know what happened.

The years after Tiananmen were particularly hard for anyone who did not stick to the proverbial government-approved script. Jiang focused on his studies. He had always been interested in the law, but his grades had not been good enough for that field, so instead he studied Chinese philology, which he also liked. He worked as a professor for ten years, from 1994 until 2004. Those were good years, as he connected with his students, and had a peaceful life. He valued liberty and justice, but in his mind, the concept of human rights did not exist. That was an intrinsically Western ideal, developed during the French Enlightenment and in liberal British schools of thought, but absent from Chinese culture.

"When did it 'click' for you?" I ask.

"When I was assigned to teach Political Education to students in the last year of secondary school. I couldn't make them learn the curriculum I was given, it was pure propaganda. So I explained to them that we would divide the class into two parts: I would teach them what was in the book so they would pass the exams; then we would talk about how things actually were in the real world," he says with a laugh.

At that time Jiang would often talk on the phone with his good friend Li Heping, who had been working as a lawyer in Beijing for the past couple of years. Li always encouraged him to change professions. "You have to take the lawyer exam," Li Heping would tell him. "That's for you. You won't get rich, but you'll be doing something important." Jiang gave it serious consideration. He thought about the writings of Robespierre and Danton that had made such an impression on him, and the French Revolution, and the American Revolutionary War. He had to do something to get the Chinese people to speak up and make their voices heard. A few months later, he resigned his teaching position, packed his suitcase and took the train to Beijing.

H is first case was a lawsuit for workplace negligence, business as usual in China. A worker from the east coast had been left blind in one eye welding at a construction site with no protection, but his employer refused to indemnify him. "The worker's family was desperate, they had been to several lawyers, but the company had paid all of them off," Jiang remembers. When he won the case, he felt there was no going back.

A few days later he got a call from Chen Guangcheng (the blind activist that he and some other lawyers had decided to go visit a few years later, right before Jiang was detained). At the time Chen was working to expose the brutal enforcement of the one child only policy[14] in certain areas of the country. He gave a horrifying description: in the Linyi district in Shandong province, local authorities were sterilizing thousands of women by force, and carrying out forced abortions on many others. Chen sounded extremely upset on the phone: "You have to come, Jiang," he implored. "The people here are terrified. They don't want to sleep in their homes because at night officials carry out raids and take away the women. They're detaining and torturing the ones who refuse to get abortions or be sterilized. They're drugging pregnant girls so they can rip the fetuses out of their wombs!"

Jiang was puzzled. "It was hard for me to believe that such savagery was going on just five hundred miles away." Without wasting any time, he and a friend set off on the highway to go see for themselves. The sun was setting when they parked their car in one of the villages Chen had told him about. "We saw it with our own eyes. We heard several residents shouting, 'They're coming! The demons are coming!'[15] Ten local officials drove into town in several vehicles. When they saw us talking with the villagers, and heard that we spoke Mandarin and not the local dialect, they got nervous and left." But the hostilities in Linyi did not stop. The regional government assured that they would take measures, but that was not the case. When some other lawyers went to offer their support to the villagers a few months later, the officials had hired some thugs to beat them up.

Jiang's caseload began to increasingly deal with politically sensitive topics one day he would represent peasants who had been forced off their land by real estate speculation; the next it was defending Falun Gong practitioners; then victims who had been infected with the HIV virus after having received tainted blood transfusions in public hospitals. "It's not that I wanted to specialize in those kinds of cases, but I wouldn't turn them down, either," says Jiang. "When you're dealing with sensitive issues, you know you're not going to earn much money, the secret police will be after you, and they'll harass you until they take away your license to practice law. And there are so few lawyers willing to do it, that in the end it's always the same group taking on the cases."

S ooner or later, he knew the Ministry of State Security would call him up and invite him to "have tea," a euphemism for a police interrogation. It usually goes something like this: the dissident or journalist gets a call from a public official who politely invites him to meet, often in a tea house. Once at the meeting, the tone can be friendly or threatening, depending on how much of a liability the individual in question represents for the government. Jiang was moving into the "undesirable" category, and they let him know it.

"It was the spring of 2005. A few days before, I had met with some other lawyers who were representing members of Falun Gong, and several government agents had followed us. When I got the call from the Ministry I knew I was in danger, but I didn't have any choice but to go. They invited me to meet with them at a tea house near my home in Beijing. When I got there we greeted each other, exchanged business cards just like you would at any business meeting, and they politely asked me what my career had been before I became a lawyer, and why did I decide to change professions," Jiang recounts. "They wanted to know how I knew the other lawyers connected to Falun Gong, and what our intentions were. I answered everything very calmly. It was the first time I had met with them, and I had decided to be open and sincere as long as they treated me with respect. I told them I wanted to contribute to the development of Chinese laws."

As the hours ticked by, the agents changed their tone.

"They told me that actually my lawyer friends had hidden agendas, that they were puppets of a foreign plot to destroy China," Jiang relates. Two pots of tea later, one of the agents pounced.

"I think the best thing would be for you to go back to teaching in Henan," he said.

Jiang was on his guard. "Is that a threat?"

"No, of course not," the police agent said. "It's just a piece of advice, because we're friends, and friends give each other advice."

There were many other meetings after that first one. Jiang noticed that government agents followed him around more as sensitive dates approached, to try to prevent him from meeting with other activists or the media. Around the anniversary of the Tiananmen massacre, they illegally placed him under house arrest. Two guards were stationed outside his door twenty-four hours a day. He was not allowed to go outside for several days, but he kept right on working. Cases of totally helpless, indigent citizens abused by the authorities continued to find their way to him. The atrocities committed by police enforcing the one-child policy in Shandong went on as before, but now no one talked about it since the Government had barred any media from entering the area. Jiang was especially troubled by the case of a twenty-eight-year-old woman left almost paralyzed by the drugs they had injected her with to sterilize her against her will.

He finally reached the point where he had to make a decision that many Chinese are faced with some point in their lives: to go against the current, or swim with it. He never doubted which course he would take.

W hile he was in custody, he had no choice but to closely examine his past. The police forced him to write hundreds of pages on what he did, his family, and his contacts. He composed entire dissertations on what books he liked, and his aspirations for the future. Everything had to be conveyed in a tone of repentance. The authorities were looking for a self-critique, not a memoir.[16]

It grew increasingly difficult to concentrate in that empty room. "I was at the end of my rope, mostly because of the sleep deprivation. Exhaustion is dangerous. Sometimes I frightened myself because I had these irresistible thoughts about banging my head against the wall, or punching the guards when they brought me food. Just when they knew I was at my weakest mentally, they ordered me to start writing."

He had to write on eight subjects, divided into sections. For example, in one he had to explain what he knew about the Arab Spring uprisings, what he thought of it and why. In another he summarized all the connections he had abroad: what embassies he knew, what diplomats and journalists he knew and what he talked about with them. And he had to write about his own reeducation, why he was being subjected to it, and what lessons he hoped to learn from it. He had to take care not to copy from other people's conclusions, his had to be entirely original.

He spent twenty days writing. When he finally finished, they ordered him to start again from the beginning because "it wasn't sincere or deep enough." He rewrote the eight subjects three times. Then they demanded that he write a five-page summary. His head was spinning. They videotaped him explaining what he had written, and why. The authorities make some dissidents renounce their ideals on camera, and later use the videos to discredit them. "Every time I said a word they didn't like, they stopped taping, and would spend the next four or five days instructing me on that particular term. For example, they asked me who the Dalai

Lama was. I answered that he was a public figure, and they were enraged. What do you mean a public figure? They said. He is the leader of a separatist group that has tried to divide China for years. He is the devil himself, how dare you say he is a public figure? I tried to take it back, but it was too late. They spent five days deconstructing the definition of public figure, the etymology, the similarities and differences between "public figure" and "leader." It was totally ridiculous, it was Kafkaesque, but they didn't stop. No matter how many times I swore to them that I understood, they kept barking out the definitions just to torture me. I thought I was going to lose my mind," he says, rubbing his temples.

Sometimes his interrogators went off on surreal tangents. "Today we're going to talk about your promiscuous tendencies. Do you love your wife?"

Jiang could hardly believe it, his torturers were acting like hosts of some trashy talk show. Trying not to offend them, he answered very sincerely that of course he loved his wife, and had never been unfaithful to her even once. The lead interrogator snapped, "That's a lie! We know you've had relations with other women! We know everything about you, and don't you forget it."

A few weeks before his release, the police agents asked what he planned to do once he got out. He knew from other dissidents that had been tortured that when they asked that question, it meant they were considering letting him go.

"Think about it, and tonight you can tell our boss," the agents said.

Jiang didn't know what to do. If he told them the truth, that he planned to continue working to ensure the laws were obeyed and do what he could to improve his country, maybe they would never let him out. As powerful as they were, sooner or later they would find out anyway. When the police chief barged into the room later as his subordinates bowed obsequiously before him, Jiang, pale, with dark circles under his eyes and greasy, matted hair clinging to his forehead, announced in terms as ambiguous as he could muster that he would continue to work to ensure that the laws were followed. The police chief frowned and left abruptly.

The guards hurried into the room. "If you continue to refuse to cooperate, how can we be happy with you?" they reproached. "How will the chief be pleased? You should have said you would cooperate with the police from now on. Haven't you thought about your family at all? How is it any fault of theirs that you're so obstinate? All you talk about is the law, the law, the law. . . . If you wanted to cooperate, the government could get you a job in an official capacity, and you'd be the boss in no time. You would earn much more money."

H e finally saw the light of day again on April 19, 2011. He doesn't know why they chose that date. His release was as arbitrary as the detainment itself, the interrogations and accusations had been. "In the last days I was very docile, I answered however I thought a reeducated person would answer. I guess it worked," he says.

His captors dropped him off at the same spot where they had taken him, covering his head with a black hood. Before they left, the police ordered him to stay in touch with them, and keep them apprised of his whereabouts, and his contacts. They reminded him it would be very easy to make him disappear, or suffer an "accident." "They forbid me from having any meetings concerning sensitive issues, unless they were *very* sensitive. Then I would have to deliver them a report," he says with a laugh.

"Now what?" I ask.

He shrugs, looking resigned. He has lost his license to practice law, and can only work as a legal advisor. He has come home only to find his front door sealed shut with silicone four times. Once in a while, someone puts an extra padlock on his wife's bicycle. His daughter is only nine years old, but she knows her family is different from the others. Jiang tells me how she came home from school one day very upset, because a police agent had gone there to ask her if she knew what her father did. He has gotten used to having his email and telephone monitored. His wife is very supportive, but she suffers from nightmares. When I ask him how he bears it, he takes his glasses off and rubs his eyes.

"This is how it is," he says. He sighs heavily and looks out the window. The sun is setting, and evening traffic clogs the streets. "Chinese activists don't do anything bad or illegal, and the proof is that other countries support us. We simply want to change the situation. If we don't do something, future generations will suffer through the same things. The fundamental problem in this country is that there's only one party. The whole system is based on the Communist Party, which manages everything, and works for the benefit of a few privileged families. The Party controls the Government, the courts, and the People's General Assembly, state-owned companies and the media. There are no independent powers. Behind the police, the media and the judges is the Party. As long as there is just one party, nothing will change. No matter who you are, even if you're a police officer, the system will crush you if necessary."

I ask if he's ever thought about going into exile. Some of his friends have done it. There are hundreds of Chinese dissidents in Europe, Australia and the United States. It's a very difficult decision to make: many feel guilty for betraying their principles, and depressed for leaving their family, friends, and country. We talk about the case of Wang Yanhai, one of the most important activists defending AIDS victims. He is one of Jiang's close friends. When I interviewed him in 2009, he had told me that he suffered from excruciating, debilitating pain in his back. He had also been tortured, and reached the point where he could not take it anymore. Very reluctantly, in May 2010 he packed his bags and took his wife and daughter to the United States. When Wang arrived in Washington, Jiang explains, he did not need to seek any medical treatment because the pain in his back disappeared. He had been suffering from the effects of pure stress.

"My wife and I have thought about it many times. If we leave, who will take care of our parents? It would be very difficult for us to come back." He gazes out the window again, and seems to be talking to himself. "I was in Holland once, and it was lovely. China used to have amazing, historic buildings, but they have been demolishing them. If we went to the United States, I know my daughter could do very well in school, not like here, where I'm a blot on her record. Yes, I know America and Europe are very beautiful places. But China could be, too."

3

A Gay Husband
Is Better Than None

T hree years ago Xiao Qiong married the love of her life, but she has never slept with him. They've never even kissed. Her husband is homosexual, and she's known it from the start. But, extremely traditional, raised to be an excellent student and then become a self-effacing wife who never raised her voice at home, she thought this gay thing was a fad that would eventually pass.

The first time we met, she was impeccably dressed. Eager to make a good impression, she wore high heels (admitting to me later they killed her feet), and a white beaded necklace that matched the pin in her hair, which she wore up in a bun. She was thirty but looked about ten years older, even though her round face still hinted at the pudgy teen she once had been. Everything about her was exceedingly proper: the way she walked, how she offered her hand in greeting, as she had seen other Westerners do (the Chinese only say hello in greeting or lightly bow if they are expected to make an exceptional show of respect), how she sat down very carefully so as not to wrinkle her skirt, and the way she told her story. We met many times before she said anything remotely improper.

Xiao Qiong is what's known as a *tongqi*,[1] which translates as "wife of a homosexual," but she never uses that word in public. It is not an offensive term, but she would be humiliated if everyone knew, because getting married is more important than anything else in life. She had dreamed about her wedding day ever since she was a little girl, and she had had her perfect ceremony planned down to the last detail. It would be at the seaside, and instead of wearing a red *qipao* (旗袍), the traditional one-piece Chinese bridal dress, she would be radiant in a white bridal gown with a long train, just like a princess or "the models in *Vogue*." In her fantasy, she would take off her shoes and dance with her husband on the sand, as the sun slowly set over the water.

That had been her plan. Ever since she was little, she had done everything she could so that one day she would be that barefoot girl on the beach, her white veil fluttering in the breeze. In the end, reality turned out to be just the opposite.

It is hard to pinpoint exactly how many *tongqi* there are in China. Rough estimates put the number at sixteen million women married to gay men, but it could be even higher. Many homosexuals live a double life, because the cost of coming out of the closet is too high. The tolerance of centuries past contrasts sharply with the hard line conservatism of the last fifty years.

References to homoerotic friendships abound in Chinese literature and history. During the Song, Ming, and Qing dynasties, as in ancient Greece, love between men was common, but was always cloaked in metaphors and ambiguity. Some poems also talk about intimate relationships among women, who would eventually be separated so they could be married. The first homophobic law was officially passed in 1740 during the Qing dynasty, but gays were not systematically persecuted until 1949, with the creation of the People's Republic. Under Maoism, gays were seen as counterrevolutionary. They had embraced a capitalist perversion, and therefore had to be eliminated. In the best of cases, they were forced to marry a woman and have children. In the worst, they were castrated, tortured, and sentenced to forced labor camps for decades. Public parks, saunas and bath houses became clandestine meeting places for gay men.

Homosexuality continued to be a crime until 1997, and it was still considered a mental illness until 2001. Today, gay men are prohibited from donating blood, because they are considered a high-risk group. There are some gay bars, support groups, and some gay fanzines, but it is a very limited sphere. To Chinese society as a whole, still deeply Confucian, getting married and procreating is an essential part of life. In rural areas, gays who refuse to marry simply to keep up appearances are vulnerable to attack. He Xiao Pei, a sexologist with the gay collective Pink Space, told me she didn't know how to help a thirty-five-year-old man from Sichuan, two thousand miles to the southeast of Beijing. He lived in a remote village and had been calling her on the phone for days, because his neighbors had found out that he was gay. He had been unable to leave his house for several months, for fear they would lynch him.

Coming out is very complicated. Very few people dare to even tell their own families the truth. As the New Year approaches, a time when families traditionally get together, pressure on single people in general mounts, but especially if they are homosexual. They know that at some point during dinner, one relative or other will ask why they're not married, and what are they waiting for. For the last several years, many gays and lesbians have found each other through special forums on the Internet. They make friends and form fake relationships to placate their families, going home to introduce their parents to their new "girlfriend" or "boyfriend" and announce their engagement. A few weeks later they may tell their families they have broken up, or they may even marry but continue to live separately, showing up as a couple to family events to keep up the charade.

X iao Qiong didn't know anything about all of this when she had been in school. As a student she had been a nerd, shy, and somewhat antisocial. All she did was study and steal furtive glimpses at Xu Bing,[2] who had big eyes and talked very softly, almost in a whisper. He drove her crazy. Every day, she tried to sit next to him and casually run into him in the hallways. They would chat in between classes, and call each other on their birthdays and on the Mid-Autumn Festival. After graduation, they went out to dinner a few times with the rest of their classmates, and at one he announced he had a girlfriend. That was the end of that. Xiao Qiong began working at a magazine in downtown Beijing, and kept on dreaming about meeting a man she could marry on the beach.

Then one day she got a phone call. It was Xu Bing. Her heart skipped a beat, although she acknowledges she would have had the same reaction hearing any male's voice on the other end of the line. At the time, the only people that ever called her were her four girlfriends and her mother.

He sounded happy. He asked her how she was doing, and if she would be able to meet him for tea that coming Friday. She told him yes, as she had nothing planned besides doing her nails and reading, but it seemed odd that he wanted to see her. They met at a UBC, a local chain where a cup of coffee cost more than a three-course dinner would at any other neighborhood restaurant.

They sat at a table upstairs, where couples usually go to have a little more privacy. Xu Bing ordered red-bean ice cream, served in a big plate over a mound of chipped ice, for the two of them to share. They were both nervous. They politely asked each other what they had been doing over the past few months, about their jobs and their families, and then they fell silent, unsure how to continue. Finally Xiao Qiong tentatively asked about the girl he had been dating. Were they still together?

Xu Bing looked at her directly and confessed he did not have a girlfriend, and in fact had never had one. Many girls from their high school had wanted to go out with him, but he had turned them down. In a word—and he gazed even more intently into Xiao Qiong's eyes—he was not interested in women.

"He spoke very deliberately, as if he was trying to gauge my reaction. After he told me that, he was quiet. Then I understood. He had always reminded me of Li Yu Gang,[3] a man with very delicate, feminine mannerisms, but who is actually attracted to women," Xiao Qiong says. We are having tea, and her hand trembles as she picks up her cup.

That afternoon, she remembers, Xu Bing talked for hours, finally having found someone to confide in. He told her how hard it had been to keep his sexual preference a secret in school. He was as traditional in his outlook as she was, and being homosexual was a tremendous burden to him. His suffering had been so intense, he had come up with a theory about his family that seemed lifted right out of a soap opera: his "confused" sexuality, as he described it to Xiao Qiong, had been the reason his parents had separated when he was born. His mother had left without leaving so much as a note, and his father had remarried a woman as cold as ice, so he had not had anyone to talk to. Xiao Qiong listened and nodded. Sitting there with him eating ice cream from the same dish was a gift, no matter where the conversation went. She didn't really understand what his mother and stepmother had to do with his sexual preference, but she comforted and consoled him, assuring him none of it was his fault.

"When we said goodbye, he thanked me, and said finally he'd be able to get a good night's sleep. That made me happy, but once I got home, I felt empty again." As she talks, Xiao Qiong nervously wrings her hands and fingers the beads on her necklace. Several locks of hair have come loose from her bun. "I couldn't sleep that night. I couldn't stop thinking about how, while I was thinking about him, he was thinking about men. And if it hadn't been for that, it would have been perfect: his father had a good job, and if we got married, we wouldn't want for anything. But he had only called me to unburden himself."

She decided to educate herself about homosexuality. She read compulsively: leaflets, novels, Web sites and chat rooms on the Internet. She wanted to understand Xu Bing. One night, she even ventured out to a lesbian bar in Beijing, just to see what it was like.

She found out that there are far more gay men in China than one would imagine, but nine out of ten of them marry women. That on the Internet, men use the number 1 to define themselves as active, and 0 as passive. That every year in the Qianmen district of Beijing, several organizations stage group weddings, as a demonstration in support of approving gay marriage rights. She learned how difficult it is to hold onto a job if anybody at a workplace discovers that someone is homosexual.

At the same time, she couldn't help but experience the usual range of emotions after a first date. Night after night she laid in bed staring up at the ceiling. She thought about Xu Bing, and how he managed to be happy. Was he happy? Did he go to those bars? Would his family know?

They saw each other again, and they opened up to each other. She described her fears to him: failure, loneliness, not being a good daughter, losing her job at the magazine. He listened closely, furrowing his brow, "as if he were solving a complex equation at the institute," Xiao Qiong relates. He told her that his father and stepmother pressured him to find a girlfriend. They shared the same existential angst typical of all Chinese who pass their twenty-fifth birthdays without any marriage prospects on the horizon.

Xiao Qiong had seen it coming. One night when she went to have dinner at her parents' house, they confessed they were looking for a husband for her. For the past several weeks they had been talking to acquaintances who had sons between twenty-five and thirty years old. "Don't get upset, daughter. They all have good jobs," her mother justified, sounding like a door-to-door salesman, a wide smile plastered across her face. Xiao Qiong sighed and continued clearing the table. She had known that sooner or later her parents would get to work on it. At least they hadn't gone down to Zhongshan Park with her resume and a picture, like many of her friends' parents had done. On the weekends, Zhongshan, near the Forbidden City, becomes a sort of open-air bazaar. Armed with all the necessary information on their offspring, including medical histories, parents gather to find them spouses. The sales pitches are straightforward marketing: "My daughter has a Masters in finance, graduated with honors, and has studied calligraphy and piano since she was four years old," a mother brandishing her daughter's photo might say. "Well, my son speaks English and Russian, and has read all of the classics. He is in excellent health, and every summer he volunteers with our neighborhood's Communist youth league." "Perfect, but does he own an apartment?" If the answer is no, the parents of the girl brusquely dismiss the young man's parents with a quick nod of the head, and look around for the next candidate.

While they are being auctioned off, the children are usually not there. If unfortunately for them they happen to witness the bartering, they skulk away dying of embarrassment, hoping that the earth might suddenly open up and swallow them whole. Xiao Qiong was glad that at least in her case the negotiations were relatively discreet. Her parents would definitely set her up with the sons of friends and acquaintances, and she would spend three or four excruciating evenings out with guys who were boring, maniacal, repellent or ugly as sin. They would talk about the weather over appetizers, and later put their cards on the table. Her date would spell out whether he owned his own apartment and car,[4] and had a residency permit in Beijing, which was essential for getting a job, going to the doctor and enrolling children in school without any hassles. They were basically business dinners. Xiao Qiong had friends that had been through the same thing, so at least she knew that she would emerge from the process with some funny stories of her own to tell.

And she shared her anecdotes with Xu Bing, who was starting to go through something similar. Although he still didn't own a home, his father was considering buying him an apartment just to increase his value in the marriage marketplace.

They shared a lot of laughs over it, and then felt guilty for trivializing their parents' feelings. In their hearts, neither one wanted to let their families down, but the ridiculous system of set-ups and blind dates struck them both as sadly pathetic. Xu Bing began to think the best thing would be to leave the country, and kill two birds with one stone: be free of the pressure to find a girlfriend, and come out somewhere other than in China. "He knew I had relatives abroad, and we joked that the best thing would be to go as far away as we could," Xiao Qiong remembers. "One day he asked if my relatives would help him get out of the country, and I replied, laughing, that if he married me they definitely would."

She doesn't remember exactly how, but marriage became a recurring topic of discussion. It was like a game, where they both imagined pleasing their families, while still being free to live their own lives independently, however they wanted.

One day, Xu Bing asked her if she could marry him and accept "his situation." Like her, he was hesitant to explicitly label things as they were. Xiao Qiong said she could. And that's when things started to snowball.

One of the biggest problems Xiao Qiong has, as she herself admits, stems from having devoured the works of Qiong Yao as a teen, Taiwan's most popular romance writer. Those stories, where a man and a woman endure all manner of suffering just to be together (usually a very bad person stands in their way), have cost her dearly.

Marrying Xu Bing represented many things for her. It meant helping out a close friend with serious problems; leaving the family nest; not feeling like a loser socially anymore; and finally having someone to rent a rowboat with in the park. But more than anything, it meant scoring a personal victory after so long, and finally reaching the happy ending to the romance novel of her fantasies.

The first discrepancies emerged when they began planning the wedding. Xiao Qiong still had the scene on the beach fixed in her head, with the fluttering veil, laughing guests, and softly glowing lights. Xu Bing wanted to sign a piece of paper. He had met someone he liked, and wanted to celebrate his liberation with his new boyfriend.

"My father-in-law told us we didn't have to complicate things, and instead of paying for a big banquet, he would rather give us money so we could travel. Xu Bing agreed that would be best, so I didn't have much of a choice," Xiao Qiong complains.

A few months before the wedding, pictures are taken. This is a time to go all-out, and couples typically spend at least a month's salary for the photo shoot. The most extravagant travel to exotic locales to have pictures taken, like the island of Hainan, or even Bali. The rest choose several outfits and pose for posterity in a studio or a park. Some classic wardrobe choices are the revolutionary uniforms that all couples had to pose in during Mao's era, Little Red Book[5] in hand. Imperial dress and Western-style gowns are also popular.

Xiao Qiong had not set her sights on traveling outside of Beijing to take the pictures. She would have been happy with a photo shoot at the Botanical Gardens, the almond trees in bloom, or at Lake Beihai, its surface covered with lotus leaves. Xu Bing did not like the idea of making a big fuss, and in the end they agreed to have the pictures taken in a photo studio.

"I will never forget that day," Xiao Qiong recalls. "It's usually the bride who chooses the type of album and the outfits. The bridegrooms just go along with it, they're tired and complain . . . that's how my friends' husbands had been. But Xu Bing got into his role right away. He was like a model. The photographer told him he had never seen such a handsome bridegroom, and there seemed to be a real spark between them. I was just there as a spectator, while he reveled in the wardrobe changes and compliments. While I got changed and they put on my makeup, he kept right on posing for the camera."

It had been humiliating to see the pictures a few days later, and confirm that many more had been taken of the bridegroom than of her. She had changed outfits five times, while he had changed six times. "He was incredibly handsome. He looked like a movie star, all the girls in the studio were saying so, and the photographer too," she remembers, biting her lower lip. She says this bitterly, but also with a trace of fascination. She did not for a moment consider calling off the wedding.

I t had been a winter morning. After signing the marriage certificate, they went to a hotel to eat, like any ordinary birthday lunch. Both of their parents were there, they were the only guests. Xu Bing observed the ritual of serving tea to his in-laws. As he poured into their cups, he proclaimed, "Father, you can rest assured. I will take care of Xiao Qiong." She felt sick to her stomach on hearing this, but she didn't say anything.

After the meal, they walked their parents to their cars. They had watched them drive away, and then Xiao Qiong and Xu Bing also parted ways. She went back to her apartment and spent her wedding night watching television and eating peanuts. He went to his boyfriend's apartment, where he has spent every night since the wedding.

X iao Qiong likes to meet for walks. Once she starts walking there's no stopping her, she can go for hours before deciding to sit down to rest. She says it relaxes her, and helps her sleep better. For months she has been drinking special infusions of herbs and roots prepared by her doctor, to help her get a restful night's sleep. But every night she has the same nightmare: she's a student again, running to get to class because she overslept, and the teacher's handing out an exam. But she hadn't known about the test, and hadn't studied for it. She wakes up bathed in sweat, calling out for Xu Bing, but she's alone in bed.

"I think I've been very stressed since the wedding," she says. "I didn't get a ring, or a honeymoon, or a proper reception, and I feel frustrated. When he didn't even spend our wedding night with me, I realized I had not gained a thing by getting married, but it was like a spiral I didn't know how to get out of." She quickens her pace. We walk down Xinjiekou, a street filled with musical instrument shops. An old man warms up a trumpet in the doorway of one shop. He is so frail, it seems he may collapse from the exertion after every note he blows. His thorax inflates and deflates like a bellows. The sun is rising in the sky, and Xiao Qiong opens her white parasol with embroidered beige trim. Like most of her countrywomen, she would hate to get a suntan.

"The worst time was a month after we got married, because Xu Bing's father got sick. We moved into his house to take care of him," she tells me. His family didn't know they lived separately, in different parts of the city, and this was the first time they would share a bed. "It was very hard, because we had to pretend all the time. So his parents wouldn't suspect anything, he only called his boyfriend from our bedroom with the door closed. I heard all their conversations. And to top it off his boyfriend was jealous because I was there: that was too much."

They managed to follow a typical Chinese couple's routine. She arrived home from work early and cooked dinner for Xu Bing and his parents. Then they all watched the news on CCTV 1 together, and if the weather was nice, they took a walk around the block to digest. "Sometimes we had a good time, because we did get along well," Xiao Qiong explains. "The problem was when the phone would ring. Xu Bing got very nervous and rushed into the bedroom, or hung up quickly. His parents didn't understand what was going on, and they would give me looks, but I didn't know what to say. It was too much pressure."

One night the tension boiled over.

"His boyfriend had picked a fight and they had argued. He took it out on me and I lost my temper. I couldn't take it anymore and I said, Listen, brother,[6] can you help me out? You're so delighted with your life you've dumped the whole problem on me. But he only thought about himself. He said, Aren't you happy? Does anyone beat you or insult you?"

By then they were screaming at each other. His parents called from the living room for them to calm down, but the snowball was racing down the hill. "They knocked on the door and pleaded with us to let them come in. His father asked what our problem was, and I said you should ask your son that, and I left. I went out for a walk, I don't remember where. By the time I got back an hour later, Xu Bing had told them."

There wasn't any drama. His parents admitted they had suspected. "They thought being homosexual was like drinking or smoking, that you could give it up if you had the willpower. They kept saying it was Xu Bing's boyfriend's fault, for leading him down the wrong path."

The philosopher Mencius[7] said that a family with no offspring is mutilated and incomplete. Xu Bing's parents were mortified by the idea of anyone finding out what had happened, and even more horrified by the prospect of not having grandchildren. Once their son and his wife had left, they breathed easy again. The situation hadn't changed, but they didn't have to face it. Everything was as it should be once again, in the eyes of their neighbors.

Xiao Qiong was happy to be back at her own place too, at least she didn't have to put on an act. Xu Bing only had a toothbrush in her bathroom. He kept on living with his boyfriend, picking her up on the weekends to make the round of visits, lunch at one set of parents' house, and dinner with the other. They spent a few hours in each home, talking about superficial things, avoiding delicate subjects, then saying goodbye until the following Saturday.

We are sitting on a park bench, drinking bubble tea. The stifling summer heat of Beijing makes her feel groggy, she says, dabbing with a tissue around her nose where small beads of sweat have formed. She is wearing a green sleeveless cotton dress, exposing her dark underarm hair. Like many Chinese, she wears little ankle socks with her sandals so her feet won't sweat.

I ask if she has ever considered trying to find a lover.

"No, never. I'm married," she replies, a little offended. She takes a sip of tea, looking down at her straw, pensive.

One thing she has done from the beginning is seek out other women in the same situation. It was as easy as typing the term *tongqi* into a search engine, and hundreds of messages and forums about women married to gay men appeared. Some are virgins, while others sleep with their husbands and have children. "They reach a kind of agreement. They are good fathers, it's just that they also have outside relationships with men," Xiao Qiong says, very serious.

She has grown very close to some other *tongqi*, although always through the Internet. Most of them are too embarrassed to meet in person. They are all around the same age, between twenty-five and thirty-five, live in cities in different provinces around the country, and have a computer, or enough money to go to a cyber-café. Xiao Qiong figures there must be thousands of *tongqi* in the countryside who don't even know that's what they are, and share a similar profile. "We are shy, a bit introverted, and very traditional," she explains.

Her friends on the Internet call her *jiejie*, big sister, because she's become a counselor of sorts to the new arrivals. Many women visit the *tongqi* chat rooms before they get married because they have doubts about their husbands. This message appeared in the portal Tongqijiayuan, one of the most popular sites:

"My husband is always downloading gay movies, and some of them are porn. He says he's just curious. Once we had a fight and I made him delete them, but I know he keeps watching them when I'm not around. He insists that our son and I are all that matter to him. What should I do? PS: our sex life is normal."

In cases like that, Xiao Qiong advises women to get out of the relationship, just the opposite of what she herself has done. "I feel guilty with some of these women because they didn't know their husbands were gay before they got married. I did. And I still decided to get married, because I liked Xu Bing. Well, and also to not be alone," she admits, staring at the ground. Then she looks up and says, "But I'll tell you something else. I think I love my husband more than other *tongqi*. They want to get divorced, but I would like to save our marriage."

A year after she got married, Xiao Qiong still had insomnia. She sometimes cried at work, and had to go to the bathroom pretending she had a runny nose so no one would notice. She started taking antidepressants. During the week, alone in her apartment, they seemed to work. She lied on the couch for hours in a daze, wrapped up in a quilt, watching television. She kept seeing Xu Bing on the weekends to visit her parents and in-laws. Then she felt a pressure in her throat and she wanted to scream.

Her parents noticed that something wasn't right, but they didn't bring it up. In China, domestic matters are taboo, to the point that, for example, domestic abuse of women is widespread, but the neighbors do not get involved or call the police. Divorce is rampant: more than five thousand couples get legally separated every day,[8] but in traditional families like Xiao Qiong's, there is still a stigma around it.

"One time my father noticed my eyes were red from crying at lunch, and after he took me aside to ask what was wrong. But before I could say anything, he warned me that, no matter what it was, we could not get divorced because it would be a disaster for both families," Xiao Qiong remembers. "I told him things weren't going well with Xu Bing, and he answered there must be a reason, and that everything can be fixed. If he was seeing another woman,

I had to talk to him and make him leave her, if he was beating me, we would have to go to some place for therapy. Anything, he said, except divorce."

She did not want to knock down the house of cards either. Her in-laws had urged her not to "out" Xu Bing, because the neighbors might stop talking to them, and he could lose his job. She told her father she would try to work things out.

"I have news. Do you want to meet for lunch?" Xiao Qiong's voice sounded even more hoarse over the phone. She wanted us to meet at the same café where she had had her first date with Xu Bing. When I got to UBC she was waiting for me at the door, her hair tightly pulled back in a neat chignon as usual, her frameless glasses resting over her ample cheeks, wearing her sandals with socks, her face freshly washed, with no makeup. The dark circles under her eyes have almost disappeared.

We sit in the upstairs part, at the very same table where she and Xu Bing had shared the bowl of red bean ice cream three years earlier. The cold breeze from the air conditioning hits her right in the back, but she doesn't want to move. A waitress with her nails painted with Hello Kittys comes to give us menus.

After the first sip of tea, Xiao Qiong clears her throat and announces, "I am getting a divorce. I decided."

She was tired of the antidepressants, sleepless nights, and having to put on a show every weekend. She finally concluded that it wasn't worth it. She didn't even have Xu Bing's companionship, since they hardly talked at all anymore. Out of loyalty to him she had not told anyone his secret, but it was time to put her life back together. The hardest part had been convincing her parents, so she resorted to a foolproof strategy: she told them her husband could not have children. Horrified by the idea of not having any grandchildren, they themselves encouraged her to divorce him.

"What does Xu Bing think?" I asked.

"I don't know. He doesn't answer the phone. I talked it over with his mother. His parents know now he lives with his boyfriend. They still think he has just lost his way and his boyfriend led him down the wrong path. They're very sad because they'll never have grandchildren. They asked me if I remarry and have a child, to please bring the baby to visit them once in a while. They said they would take care of him like he was a member of the family."

She still loves Xu Bing, but now her concept of love has little to do with romance novels. Now she is more pragmatic. She worries about having to take care of her parents when they're old all by herself, and about being childless at thirty. But she'd rather take her chances than keep on pretending. "I read this the other day. A married couple spends an average of fifty years together. That's 18,250 days," she tells me. "I'm not going to spend all that time like this. I wrote my friends on the Internet and told them it was finished, that soon I'll be an ex-*tongqi*."

4

✦✦✦✦✦

Silence: The Master Speaks

His students told me where I could find Master Du, a kung-fu[1] legend. He would be willing to spend time with me, they said, but under no circumstance should I talk to him while he was training. "Don't even say 'hello', because that would break his concentration," warned Xiao Ma, who had begun training with Master Du three years earlier.

I went to see him at seven in the morning. The sun was already high in the sky, since it rises at four in the summertime. For political reasons, China has only one time zone, although because of its size it really should have three. A storm the night before had left the air fresh and humid. The sound of a military march floated on the breeze, as students at a nearby school performed their morning calisthenics outside to drums and trumpets.

Master Du and his students meet outside of the Worker's Gymnasium, a storied athletic institution in Beijing. Construction was completed in 1961. It was built as a covered stadium to host the world Ping-Pong championships, in what was then the outskirts of the city. Except for high-level officials, almost everyone came to the matches on their bicycles. Now the neighborhood is considered part of central Beijing. The Gymnasium mostly hosts pop concerts, and on the weekends no one can park around it. It was here in December 2011 the first Mandarin version of *Mamma Mia!*, the musical inspired by the ABBA song, was staged.

The first traffic jam of the day had taken root in the streets around the Gymnasium. Hundreds of cars and bicycles, most of them electric, snaked around each other on the unmarked pavement. Poor peasants pushed carts full of fresh leeks and carrots to sell at the market. One had set up a little stand selling watermelons beside the Gymnasium entrance. You know summer in Beijing has begun when you start seeing watermelon stands popping up everywhere.

The grounds around the stadium were still damp. On a patch of shaded lawn off in the distance, a man repeatedly struck the trunk of a poplar tree, his arms extended out, as if he were chopping it down. He looked straight ahead, his back straight, his legs bent slightly. Whack, whack, whack. He hit it cleanly, with unusual strength, so forcefully that someone without proper training trying the same thing would have destroyed their forearms. He looked to be around fifty years old, but he was actually over seventy. It was Master Du.

His students watched in silence. When the master paused, they would approach him to ask if he needed anything. They waved mosquitoes away from him, and offered tea and cigarettes. Wearing a white silk uniform and spotless white slippers, the older man declined their offers and continued with his training. He circled around the tree like it was an opponent, dodging and weaving as if to evade imaginary blows.

After an hour he was finished. Eyes closed, he breathed deeply, his abdomen rising and falling. His youngest student, twenty-five-year-old Xiao Ma, took his arm to help him sit down on a small folding chair. He placed a thermos of tea down next to him, lit a cigarette and offered it to him. The master took a few drags in silence, and then described the exercise he had just done.

He had come to the world of kung fu very late, when he was thirty years old, even though he had seen people practicing it ever since he was a boy. His native city, Wen An in the Hebei province, is the cradle of *baguazhang* (八卦掌), one of what are known as the internal martial arts.[2] It was first practiced in the nineteenth century during the Qing dynasty,[3] and requires very intense concentration. Du Shufeng, as he was known until he became a master, grew up in an environment far removed from martial arts. Neither he nor any of his five brothers could go to school, because they had to work. Their job was to distribute water, and they went door to door with large jugs lashed to their bicycle. By nightfall he was exhausted, and didn't have any energy left for sports.

His life changed course one summer, with unusually torrential rains. At first, the people of Wen An thought it was just a typical downpour that would force them to hunker down inside for a few hours. But it rained and rained, one day after another. Vegetable gardens flooded over, animals died, and the townspeople did not know what to do in the face of the endless rain. Du's parents closed up their house and moved to Beijing, ready to take whatever jobs they could find.

That's how Du Shufeng arrived in the capital as a young man. It wasn't hard to find work as a road worker while he waited to be called up for military service. When he got out of the service, and with his credentials from the People's Liberation Army, he got a job at Shougang steelworks. Founded in 1919, Shougang iron and steel plant was one of the shining examples of Chinese industrial development during Mao's tenure, and grew to employ 200,000 workers.

It was mind-numbingly monotonous work. To kill their boredom, the men did exercises between the machines during their breaks. "I just wanted to stay in shape, but my coworkers kept telling me I was very fast and flexible, and I should really try martial arts," Du tells me. One of them offered to introduce him to his kung-fu master. The next day, before going to work at the steel mill, they both went to Tuanjiehu Park. Du was transfixed, watching the kung-fu master move as agile as a cat. He humbly asked if he could be his student. "I said, I am old to be a beginner, but I will train very hard, harder than anybody else," he remembers.

I n Chinese culture, the role of the master is more akin to a father than a teacher. He not only instructs his disciples, he protects them, and considers them part of his family. The student shows his master the utmost respect. Student and master both have to exert the maximum effort, and it is a life-long obligation. It is a quintessentially Confucian attitude. To Confucius, the hierarchical relationship between master and disciple was one of the five pillars of a harmonious society, along with the relationships between the governor and the governed, father and son, older brother and younger brother, and husband and wife.

Master Du trained with Master Yong, eighty-five years old, and Master Jia, ninety, and would be their disciple until death. He venerates them more than his own deceased father, and never lets a New Year pass without bringing them a good bottle and a red envelope with a customary cash gift. "They are not my friends. We don't talk about personal issues. I know they are both married and have children, but I don't know anything else about their personal lives. I would never joke with them about women. We only talk about martial arts, but they are part of my family."

He began studying with Master Yong, an expert in *mianzhang*, an external martial art[4] characterized by explosive, quick blows, requiring exceptional strength and flexibility. He trained almost every day for ten years, until he met Mr. Jia. "He came up to me in the park and started doing exercises next to me. We sparred and of course he beat me. He was much better than me. His specialty was *neijiaquan*,"[5] Du recalls. "Ever since I met my masters I've never stopped practicing kung fu. It's a way of life, a way of prolonging good health." He raises his T-shirt, flexes his abdominal muscles and punches his stomach. "Look at me, I don't look my age because I'm healthy. It's not about ability, it's about internal strength. No matter how much kung fu you know, if your health is poor it won't do you any good. For young people it builds up their endurance, and allows them to work much more. For older people like me, it helps us avoid certain illnesses and stay in shape."

Tired of the folding chair, he sits on the ground, crossing his legs in the lotus position. He hardly has any wrinkles, except for a couple of lines across his forehead and around his large ears. He keeps smoking even in that position. Xiao Ma, one of his disciples, keeps lighting up cigarettes for him.

"The Master really likes to smoke," the young man muses as Du explains a technique to another student. "We can't tell him to quit. He's never in a bad mood, but when he runs out of cigarettes he gets furious."

Chinese martial arts seek a harmonious balance between the body and spirit, the interior (circulation of energy) and the exterior (movements of the body). There are dozens of different schools and styles, but they all combine physical and mental training. For example, tai chi, the Western term for *taijiquan* (太极拳), is based on circular movements around an axis point. Experts say one must flow like a river's current: one can move faster or slower, as long as it is continuous. Complete mental focus is essential, to release the energy and find balance.

Master Du's specialty is *xinyi* (形意), and he tells me it is a martial art invented by the Hui, a Muslim group in China, in the twelfth century.[6] To protect their community's interests, for eight hundred years revealing the techniques to other ethnic groups was strictly forbidden. After the 1940s the culture of secrecy relaxed, and masters and variations on *xinyi* began cropping up in different regions around the country. To the uninitiated, the most striking aspect of the style is that it incorporates the movements of ten different animals: the chicken, the dragon, the tiger, the snake, the horse, the monkey, the falcon, the bear, the swallow, and the common snipe, a migratory bird with a large beak and amazing endurance.

"If we want to learn from the horse, we should ask ourselves what abilities it has. It's true that it is very fast, but what matters to us is not how much it runs, but how it stamps its hoof before biting," Du explains, looking around at his audience. He rolls up his pants and lifts his right leg over the head of a student, who observes motionlessly. "The one thing we should not do is use kung fu to hurt someone. If we are a tiger or a lion, we also have to know how to be a sheep. And we must know how to control ourselves, because a blow can be much more potent in the internal martial arts. The force that comes out of us is very powerful."

Several older people playing checkers on the sidewalk pause their games to come over and watch what's going on. Within seconds, Master Du physically transforms: he starts to zigzag, taking little hops and flexing his neck muscles, his chin tucked into his chest. "When we think of the snake, what does the snake do before attacking? Watch. It approaches, and when it sees that it can succeed, it pounces and never lets go of his prisoner.... Bam!" The students widen the circle and jostle each other to get a good view of their master, who twists and turns in the air like a very agile teenager. When he changes animal forms, he alters his movements and his breathing. Every once in a while he makes a deep, loud gargling sound and spits. The ground around him is dotted with it.

"*Xinyi* is not any better than other martial arts form. It all depends on the practice, the effort. We use several different types of strikes," he continues. He gestures to Lao Fu, a disciple around forty years old, who enters the center of the circle and takes off his shirt. All eyes are on him. "This is the cutting, hatchet style," Lao Fu says, and strikes the air with the edge of his open hand. "There's also the sharp style, where the arm is used like a spade." Then, he extends his arm out and strikes the air in a circular motion, as if his hand were a medieval ball attached to a chain: "This is a continuous blow, where I strike my opponent without stopping." Du looks on approvingly. Lao Fu is one of his best students, even though he has only been training for fifteen years. He had had a hard time finding a master who would take him on as a student when he began his kung-fu practice, because he wasn't in the best shape physically. Du accepted him because he could relate to his late arrival to the martial arts.

"Each one of these blows corresponds to one of the five elements: earth, water, wood, metal and fire. And they also correspond to different organs in the body: the heart, liver, lungs, kidneys and spleen. That's why, when we use these five movements, we are speaking with our body," the master explains. He has been training for two hours, and not a hair is out of place. He styles it with gel, and has it parted to the side. He does not dye his hair, unlike many Chinese men, but he still looks like a dashing leading man in the movies.

I ask him what he thinks about while he trains. "I just think about my movements," he replies. "The mind controls movement and respiration. It is a circle. If you don't concentrate, the *qi* will not flow through your meridians."

In Chinese medicine, *qi* is the flow of energy, and the meridians are like the body's highways through which the energy travels. The body is a network of channels or meridians that empty out into the organs. When a person is healthy, it is because the energy flows; if it is blocked, then illness occurs. To put it simply, if, for example, one's shoulder hurts, according to Chinese medicine it is because there is a blockage of energy, as if a pipe were clogged, and it has to be unblocked in order for the *qi* to continue flowing and maintain a healthy balance.

Master Du is particularly sensitive to the subject of illness. When he was fifty-two, his first wife died suddenly of a cerebral hemorrhage. He was left with three children and an aching emptiness. He doesn't like to talk about it, and will only say that martial arts kept him from going under. At the time he was starting to train his first students, and they kept him occupied.

"Thanks to kung fu, I'm in better shape than other people my age. But when one gets old, there's nothing else to do but give in to the passage of time," he says, and spits again.

His students react. "But what do you mean, Master? None of us can beat you. You have taught us how to move. If it wasn't for you, we wouldn't even know how to kick a pebble," Xiao Ma says earnestly.

In Chinese society, humility is an essential quality. They believe that if someone is fully satisfied with himself, then he ceases being open to learning and improving himself. To demonstrate their humility, they tend to play down their own importance and denigrate themselves in public. Sometimes these displays are so exaggerated, a Westerner unfamiliar with the code might think they are insincere or have very low self-esteem, but it is simply a ritualized courtesy. Master Du would never talk about how good he is, in fact just the opposite. So his students have to contradict him to give the whole picture and provide him with what is known as *gei mianzi* (给面子, or positive reinforcement.

Xiao Ma is more devoted to his kung-fu master than anything else. He's had a rough life, having moved to Beijing from a central province two years earlier, working like a dog and sending all his money home. At first, all he could afford to do in his free time was take walks around the city. One day on one of his walks, he saw Master Du training. "It's not easy to find someone with such great *xinyi* technique," Xiao Ma explains. "People practice it very differently depending on what province they're from. The style practiced in Henan has nothing to do with the style in Anhui or Shanghai. I wanted to learn it ever since I was a child, but the schools were very expensive and I didn't have a teacher. It's a great honor for me to have been accepted as his student."

He never had to talk about money with Du. If he had brought it up, his master would have been offended, since he's of the old school and believes money corrupts the learning. "If someone wants to be my student, I ask that he have a strong will, and consider that he'll have to spend many hours training. You can't learn kung fu right away, and I can't teach someone who doesn't have any time," Du emphasizes. He doesn't like indecisive types, according to his students. He fully commits himself to the task, and expects the same from his disciples.

Xiao Ma vowed that he would spend every free minute he had training and improving. "He observed me for weeks before accepting me," he remembers. Du wanted to see what kind of person he was first. In the martial arts, moral character is just as important as physical ability. A good master's mission is not just to teach proper technique, but to instill a whole way of life. If a student turns out to be impetuous, hot-headed or foolish, it will be very hard for him to follow the *wu de*, the martial arts moral code.[7]

There's a Chinese proverb that says: A student spends three years searching for a master, and a master spends three years examining the student.

Xiao Ma's initiation ceremony was simple, and very emotional for him. At a park at daybreak, he approached Master Du, bowed deeply three times, saying "shifu," master. That night, Xiao was giddy with happiness. He sent messages to all his friends in his hometown to tell them about it.

Master Du has about a dozen disciples who are utterly devoted to him. If they all go to a restaurant, they won't let Du pay for anything. At parties and for special occasions, they give him gifts of fruit, rice liquor, and a red envelope with money, just as Du still does for his elderly masters. If they see that his clothes look thread-bare, they buy him new ones. And if they can't afford to buy him gifts, they show their gratitude in other ways. Xiao Ma has little money to spend, but he is always ready to repair Master Du's bicycle whenever he needs it. Every now and then, Xiao Ma will pay his master a visit at home, in case he needs a light bulb changed or to unclog a drain. And he has become Master Du's personal secretary of sorts, because the old man doesn't have a phone. Whenever anyone wants to talk to Master Du, they call Xiao Ma, and he personally delivers the message.

In the spring of 2011, Master Du's students arranged a surprise for him. The Martial Arts Association of Heilongjiang, a northeastern province bordering Russia, invited Master Du to come visit for several days, so they could honor him. The Association would cover train fare and lodging for him and a companion. Xiao Ma could not afford to take the time off of work, so Lao Fu, nearing retirement age, volunteered to go along.

I saw them when they came back from the trip. Master Du was radiant, but exhausted. "He hasn't trained for three days, and has been sleeping a lot," Xiao Ma told me over the phone before we met. "Don't ask him too many questions because he gets tired."

I didn't have to. Du started talking right away about what a great time he had had. "There were hundreds of people, the best masters and students in China. We talked about the spirit of kung fu, we sparred, there were presentations. Everybody wanted to take me out to fancy restaurants, but I didn't want to go. I don't like to spend anybody else's money," he affirmed.

Lao Fu added smoothly, "The Master is very modest, so he hasn't mentioned how everyone at the event wanted to see him fight. They were amazed to see how quick and agile he was, in spite of his age. They were friendly fights, no one got hurt. We had a wonderful time, but he got very tired, so we came back two days ahead of schedule, right, Master?"

Master Du grumbled, "I'm not smart, I'm uncultured. I can barely read and write. If you put a text in front of me, I'm sure there would be many characters I wouldn't understand." He asked for another cigarette, and after the second drag he had a coughing fit. Xiao Ma looked on, worried. "We went to the doctor[8] last night, and he said he's just worn out from the strain of the trip. His blood pressure has gone up. He should not have gone out today, but we had made plans to meet you and he didn't want to miss it."

"There were some very dedicated young people," the Master continued, as if he hadn't heard Xiao. "They train very hard. In the big cities like Beijing, they're more interested in having a good time. For every three hours of training, they spend two-and-a-half chatting with each other," he lamented. "In the north, conditions are better because there's more money. . . . They have so much space to train! They fight in a huge forest, among the trees, feeling the fresh breeze, the earth under their feet. It's very nice. And they've built a covered patio, two thousand square feet, so they can keep training when it rains. In Beijing we have a different rhythm. We never hear silence anymore."

When Master Du first started training near the Workers Gymnasium, there were no tall buildings around it, just fields. Now, he trains with his students on a patch of grass surrounded by a bowling alley, several nightclubs, and restaurants open twenty-four hours. Martial arts aficionados complain about the lack of green space in the city. In theory, they are supposed to train in close contact with the earth, but in recent years many fields have been paved over because of the real estate boom. Some parks are still left, but Beijing's landscape has changed radically. Over the course of just six months, a street can become unrecognizable. Some call the city the Chicago of the twenty-first century.

M aster Du acknowledges that, although he doesn't like the city as much as he did years ago, at least pollution levels have gone down. When he first arrived in Beijing, the factories were going full blast, burning massive quantities of coal and expelling thick clouds of black smoke that stuck in your throat. In the Shijingshan neighborhood, where the Shougang steel plant was located, the women who lived nearby couldn't hang their clothes outside to dry because they would turn black with soot. "I would ride my bike home from work every day down Chang An Avenue, my face covered in black dust and coughing like a dog."

China consumes more energy than any other country in the world, and its demand is growing at an unsustainable rate. China's oil and gas reserves are limited, and they rely on coal, the most polluting fuel, for 70% of their energy needs. The government is under pressure from the international community to reduce levels of harmful emissions, which also come with a high price tag. In 2005, China spent or lost revenue worth 112 billion dollars, in health costs and lost productivity.[9]

The government's official goal is to reduce emissions by 30% by 2020, through reforestation, taking old gas-guzzling vehicles off the road, and shutting down energy inefficient factories located in city centers.[10]

The last factory to close in Beijing was the Shougang steel plant, where Master Du had worked. In 2010, the plant was relocated to an artificial island in the Bohai Bay, 125 miles to the east of the capital city, to take advantage of the close proximity to the sea and lower transportation costs.

Shutting down factories has made a noticeable difference in central Beijing. For the past few years, the sky actually looks blue for many more days per year. But this doesn't mean levels of pollution have been reduced down to zero. In recent months, Beijing has begun measuring quantities of particulate matter in the air, the smallest particles of contaminants that until 2012 had only been measured by a U.S. embassy office. The public's growing dissatisfaction with the pollution pressured the government to perform more detailed, exacting analyses of air quality.[11]

Master Du wryly observes, "The government is investing in cleaning up the environment, but once they do, there won't be any grass left to protect."

For a week, Master Du didn't leave his house, because his blood pressure had gone up following the martial arts summit in Heilongjiang. Every morning, Xiao Ma brought him breakfast: *zhou*, or rice porridge with vegetables, a popular staple in the north, and soy milk. When I called him to ask how Du was doing, he suggested we both go to visit him after lunch. "His wife would like to invite you to tea. She has never talked to a foreigner, so she's curious."

Du lives in a *xiaoqu*, a group of residential buildings no more than four stories high built around a central courtyard and separated from the street by a gate. He moved there in 1970 with his first wife. They were among the privileged few who were granted such a large apartment by the State. It took him over an hour to pedal on his bicycle to work at the factory or to his childrens' school, but he preferred living there instead of in a tiny downtown apartment.

After his wife's death, Master Du threw himself into kung fu more than ever. His eldest son was at the University by then, and his two daughters were in high school, so he devoted all of his free time to training. Concerned for him, his friends kept on encouraging him to go out with women so he could rebuild his life with someone. They set him up with Feng Xiulan, a coworker at the factory, six years his junior, who had lost her husband and was a mother of two teenage children. They got married a few months later.

As we walked across the stone-paved courtyard, Xiao Ma explained that in the fifties, these kinds of residential developments with shared outdoor space were considered luxury housing. For the residents, the common areas are just as important as their private apartments. Every chance they can, they go out to the courtyard to get some fresh air, play dominoes, gossip, hang their laundry out to dry on clothes lines tied between the trees, and eat sunflower seeds. The children play together outside until their parents call them in to wash up or eat dinner.

Three elderly men sat on a bench, basking in the sun with their birds. In Beijing, people like to take their pet birds out for a walk of sorts, covering their cages with a blanket so they don't get disoriented. When they set the cage down, they take the blanket off. Those birds on the bench were so happy in the sunlight; they chirped and sang the whole while.

We climbed three steep flights of stairs, groping along the walls since the light bulbs had burned out. Outside their apartment door, there was a red cushion with a pattern of different colored bears, and two bags of trash. Mrs. Feng, who looked to be about twice the size of Master Du, answered the door.

"What big eyes!" she exclaimed, beckoning us in. Xiao Ma chuckled.

The apartment had a cement floor. Off of a very narrow hallway were a living room, kitchen and bedroom. There were no private bathrooms, which are relatively new in China. The couple used the communal bathrooms around the corner, and a basin in the kitchen to bathe.

Master Du was in the living room, sitting atop a high bed. He smiled as we came into the room. "Sit down, sit down. It smells bad because it's so humid," he apologized immediately. Xiao Ma stepped over to the wall and sniffed it. "Yes, it's damp. Tomorrow I'll go to the market and try to find something that could fix it, Master, don't worry."

The screens in the windows had holes in them, and were starting to curl up like medieval parchment paper. Du stood, and smoothed his hair with his fingers. He seemed pleased to have visitors. "Come on, I'll show you around," he said. "It's old, but when we first moved in, it was one of the most luxurious developments in Beijing. The ceilings are over ten feet high; they don't build them like that anymore. And we have a washing machine, television, video player, heat and air conditioning. Look, look," he led me into the kitchen, full of pots and pans. He opened a drawer and took out the remote control for the air conditioner. He wanted to turn it on so we'd be comfortable, but Xiao Ma convinced him we didn't need it, so he wouldn't run up his electric bill.

"We live well," Master Du assured me, as he opened another drawer. He kept his stash of cash inside a pair of white gloves, like the kind magicians wear. The gloves were stuffed with 50 and 100 yuan notes, rolled very tightly. "We don't need this money. I keep it around just in case, but I have everything I want. The pension from Feng Xiulan isn't very much, 300 yuan a month [45 dollars], but I get 2,700 [416 dollars] and that's more than enough for us to live on. When I go out with my students, I don't pay for anything. And they always serve me the best food," he said proudly.

Mrs. Feng was pudgy and cheerful, with a short, teased hairstyle. She opened up a round, folding table, boiled some water on the stove and prepared some jasmine tea. First, she poured some in a glass, and emptied it into a plastic waste basket on the floor. "The first pour of tea tastes the worst," she explained. Then she served us all a glass.

Master Du did not drink his tea. He climbed atop his bed, and sat cross-legged, leaning his back against the wall. After a while he unbuttoned his shirt, exposing his hairless chest and rock-hard abs. "He likes to sit there and let his mind go blank," Xiao Ma commented. He always felt drowsy after meals, from the effects of the rice liquor.

His wife continuously offered us something to eat. She brought a bowl from the kitchen filled with walnuts, raisins, and little honey cakes, and set it down in the center of the table. She looked at us expectantly, smiling broadly until we tried something. "Those are my daughters," she said, gesturing toward the armoire. There was a photo affixed to one of the doors with dark red tape. "They live on the outskirts of Beijing, and they're both married. One has two children, the other doesn't have any yet. My husband also has two daughters who are both mothers, and a son. Between the two of us, we have five children and four grandchildren. Not bad, eh?"

The room was thick with heat, without any ventilation. Xiao Ma wiped the sweat from his brow with a tissue. Dots of sweat began to appear on Mrs. Feng's blouse, under her arms and just below her voluminous breasts. She asked us if we were warm, and to be polite we said we were fine. She turned on the air conditioner anyway, and let out a contented sigh as the rush of cool air hit her.

As Master Du dozed off, she asked about my family, my health, and my marital status. Once this information was processed, she wanted to know if they ate rice in my country.

When he woke up, Du showed us some pictures from the kung-fu event in Heilongjiang. Mrs. Feng couldn't find her glasses, and Xiao Ma described every image to her in minute detail. "This is a picture of the President of the Martial Arts Association in Jilin; here is a shot of the students of the regional school in Heilongjiang," he narrated patiently.

Then Master Du reached under the bed and pulled out a crumpled paper bag, as two cockroaches scurried away across the floor. Inside the bag was his most precious treasure: photos of his son, his firstborn child. It seemed to bring up painful memories, as his demeanor changed noticeably. "He's not Chinese anymore, he became American," he explained bitterly. "He doesn't want to be called by his name anymore, Du Lin. He says his name is Jason." His prodigal son was forty-one years old, and for the past ten years had lived in New York. His father did not know his street address, or which university he had attended. He only had his phone number. "Maybe you'll recognize the university," he said, showing me a picture of a young man with a square jaw, dressed in the traditional cap and gown worn at American graduation ceremonies. He was throwing his cap into the air, looking up at the sky, smiling. In the background, at the entrance to the institution, there was a coat of arms with an inscription in Latin.

"This is it," Master Du insisted, his finger touching the letters in the picture. I explained that it wasn't the name of the university, but a motto in Latin that was supposed to inspire and motivate the students. He nodded, dejected. He had been waiting for years for the chance to ask someone who could read the Latin alphabet exactly which university had graduated his son.

The subject was obviously a delicate one. Xiao Ma lowered his gaze when his master started to say how embarrassing it was that his son had barely set foot on Chinese soil in a decade, and that to reenter the country, he had to request a special visa. He had hoped that his son would graduate from a good school, but then return to China to start a family. From what I could gather, his son had not accepted his father's second marriage. In spite of this, Mrs. Feng seemed to be very proud of her stepson. She took a cardboard box out of the armoire filled with even more photos, dotted with mosquito droppings. Jason at a lake. Jason with three foreign friends at an old tea house in Beijing. Jason posing happily at the Temple of Confucius.

"He lives in America, and every once in a while he calls us. He works very hard," Mrs. Feng explained. "It's normal. Our children have their own lives. My daughters visit us when they can, but sometimes I tell them not to come and to just relax, they work too much. As long as we don't really need them, I don't want to be a burden."

The sun was setting as we left. Through the Du's window, the rooftops were bathed in a hazy yellow light, the air thick with fog and pollution. Xiao Ma still had to go back to the flat he shared with other workers to do his laundry. It was the first day off he had had in three weeks, and after washing his clothes by hand (they didn't have a washing machine), he would watch a movie on his roommate's computer. As we carefully made our way down the dark stairway, he told me about how talking about Jason always made his master sad. In 2005, he had decided to go visit him. His son bought him a ticket to New York, and helped him with the visa application. A few days before his flight, Master Du started to feel sick, and canceled the trip. Xiao Ma didn't fully understand why. It seemed that he may have been panicked by the idea of flying. He hadn't wanted to try again, and that had widened the distance between father and son even further.

A five minute walk from Master Du's home, there are bars and cafes where international literary festivals are celebrated and books banned by the Department of Propaganda are sold, and there are of-the-moment fusion restaurants which double as clothing boutiques. Du has never set foot in this consumerist section of Beijing, open to the world. He only leaves his house to go to the Workers Gymnasium to train. His wife buys their produce at a stand where two pounds of onions cost thirty cents. They sell for nine times that at the Western-style supermarket a hundred yards away.

As the neighborhood has become more fashionable, the cost of living has gone up. Many locals have had to give up meat, since the cost of pork has doubled over the course of just a few months. Some businesses have had to close because their rents have tripled. Street vendors don't want to run the risk of having the police confiscate their merchandise, so there are far fewer fruit stands around than there used to be, they know where they're not wanted. Mrs. Feng complained that the neighborhood had changed completely. She was a little worried about getting lost, but she confided she was dying to check out the area. I suggested we go on a walk together, and then I'd take them out to dinner.

When I went to pick them up they were already downstairs standing at the front entrance, neatly dressed, and seemed a little nervous. He was wearing one of his silk suits with buttons covered in blue and gray fabric, and spotless white slippers. She wore a brown cotton blouse with a floral pattern. She smelled of lavender, and carried a folding fan in her hand. I asked them where they would like to go. "Oh, anyplace at all is just fine," they replied politely.

Mrs. Feng took short steps as she walked, swaying lightly from left to right. Master Du, cigarette in hand, walking a bit ahead of her. He crossed the avenues without looking, but she anxiously clutched my forearm. "This is horrible," she murmured, as we passed by a skyscraper that spiraled upward. "How frightful to live somewhere so high up." She squeezed my arm. "How frightful, right?" she shouted so her husband would hear her over the noisy clatter of a jackhammer and the honking car horns. Master Du looked at her, shrugged and said, "That's how things are. To each his own." And he kept walking.

We turned a corner, and it was as if we had stepped back in time. We went down a *hutong* (traditional side alley) where the sounds of construction work and traffic faded away, and all that we heard was an occasional ringing bicycle bell or a radio through an open window. The ground was bare dirt, and few businesses had a door. In the middle of the narrow street, a barber shaved the nape of an elderly man's neck. He carried the tools of his trade in a plastic bin, including an old transistor radio. Beyond them, a baker rolled balls of Chinese bread. A skinny girl stuffed them with vegetables or ground pork. Master Du said hello, and the man raised a flour-covered hand.

"This is where I buy my breakfast in the morning, on the way to the Workers Gymnasium," he explained, as we continued on our way. "They are good people, from Anhui province. He has two children who help him. His wife can't because she has heart disease," Du went on. "That's how Beijing was when I first got here: there were small businesses, and we all knew each other. But *meibanfa*,[12] you can't do anything about it, the years go by, things change," he observed philosophically. "I'm hungry. Let's go eat."

Mrs. Feng chose a *huoguo* or "hot pot" restaurant. A very typical establishment in the northern regions, every table has its own burner. Diners order a pot with broth and raw ingredients that get cooked right there. It wasn't the best weather for eating *huoguo*, but Mrs. Feng was excited about going there because a neighbor had told her the food was very good, so it was settled.

The dining room was huge, with fluorescent lighting. The waitress told us that aside from *huoguo*, their specialty was seafood. A large rectangular fish tank held dozens of crabs and swimming fish. There were a couple of suspiciously motionless carp floating around in it, their eyes bulging. The waitress showed us to a table for eight in the upstairs dining room, so the Dus would be most comfortable. We ordered a two-sided pot, with one half filled with spicy broth, the other half mild, and a little of everything to cook in it: mushrooms, lettuce, radishes, chunks of pork and veal, chicken hearts, tofu, fish balls and calamari. Mrs. Feng ordered her favorite soft drink, made of almond milk, called Lulu. The Master would have his customary rice liquor.

Every time she served herself from the pot, Mrs. Feng would put some in my bowl too. She was a quintessential Chinese mother, demanding and charming. She coaxed me to try the Lulu, she cut up a piece of calamari for me, and she insisted that they turn on the air conditioning because, according to her, her husband and I were very hot. Master Du smiled. He barely ate a thing, but he drank an impressive amount of rice liquor, finishing off almost an entire bottle by himself.

At the table next to us, a young couple laughed raucously, they were a bit tipsy. The young man was trying to pick a fish ball out of the pot, but couldn't manage it. "I don't like these young people," Master Du grumbled softly. "They're always thinking about having fun, never thinking about trying hard."

Mrs. Feng swatted his shoulder playfully. "Don't get upset, old man.[13] You're always going off about the same thing. The young people do work and try hard, but times have changed. What do you want, would it be better if they marched off to the factories like we did? But you're an old man, you don't understand."

"Yes, I'm old, but the young ones can't beat me in a fight," Master Du joked, his eyes bloodshot from the rice liquor. "Youth passes, and fewer and fewer of them understand kung fu," he said. "Have you understood any of it?" he asks me. Before I could answer, he pronounced, "Surely you haven't, and even if I explained it a thousand times you'd never understand, because kung fu shouldn't be described, it must be felt. It is not a movement, it is something alive. The kung fu of some of my students is no worse than mine. They can even execute more moves than I can."

Mrs. Feng pulled away the glass in front of him. "You've had enough to drink, old man. We're going home to get some rest." We ask for the check, and he looks it over carefully. Master Du takes out his white glove full of money to pay, but I insist they let me take care of it. Mrs. Feng and I help Du down the stairs, as he was stumbling a bit. "You can call us *ayi* and *shushu*,"[14] Mrs. Feng told me as we said goodbye. "Come over anytime to have tea."

5

◆◆◆◆◆

Plunging into the Sea of Business: China's Entrepreneurs

T he spotlight rests on her, highlighting her trim figure, and the audience breaks out in thunderous applause. Some jump to their feet, clapping enthusiastically. Pausing for effect, Yang Lu smiles, picks up the microphone and greets the hundreds of people who have come to hear her advice on corporate leadership. "Good evening ladies and gentlemen. It is a great honor to be here." The audience, comprised of high-level business executives, singers, models, and the biggest names in the Beijing world of entertainment respond with another round of applause. A violinist plays on stage. Three large screens behind Yang Lu project images of purple flower petals raining down, the official color of her corporate empire. This slender, determined woman became a self-made millionaire giving seminars on how to form corporate teams and motivate them, and speaking about innovation. Only thirty years ago, before the Chinese economy opened up, this would have been unthinkable. As Yang Lu puts it, she specializes in teaching business leaders to be more "sophisticated." She combines seminars on pure management fundamentals with other workshops on the finer points of wine, coffee and golf, and other imported pleasures that help break the ice at corporate meetings. And she offers executives guidance on how to keep their professional and personal lives separate, a concept which is still very new in China.

"Today we will learn how to appreciate a nice cup of coffee, a beverage not typical of our country, but which has become very common among people like us," Yang Lu explains, pointing with a remote control to the hundred-fifty inch screen behind her. It fills with vibrant blues and yellows as Van Gogh's painting *Café Terrace at Night* appears. "The French sit in places like this to socialize over a cup of coffee. It is part of their relaxed, romantic lifestyle. In China, we want to combine professional success with moments like that," she says, and gestures toward the café tables set on the cobble-stoned street in Arles depicted in the painting. Then a new image appears. She expounds upon the origins of coffee and its many variations, in Indonesia, Jamaica, Colombia, Costa Rica, and Yemen. Transfixed, the audience listens as she tells the story of the *Lan Shan*, the Blue Mountains of Jamaica, and how their microclimate infuses the coffee beans with a unique flavor. Some take notes, and others record the presentation on their cell phones.

The violinist segues into a new melody. A blue spotlight falls on two waiters who have taken the stage to prepare different kinds of coffee. They shake cocktail shakers, set liquors aflame and top off glasses with dollops of whipped cream as Yang Lu presents the drinks to the crowd. "This is called Irish Coffee, and you don't drink it in a cup, but in a glass, because it has whiskey in it. Here we have a Viennese coffee, which is perfect for serving with dessert because of the cream, although it may be too sweet for some people. This one here is called mocha, it proves that coffee and chocolate perfectly complement each other."

Once the presentation is over, the lights come up again and everyone applauds appreciatively. "China has so much to offer, and so much to learn. Thank you all very much. I wish you good health. *Wanshiruyi!*"[1] she exclaims ceremoniously, observing Chinese protocol. The audience stands for her closing remarks. The screens fill with the radiant face of their hostess, plump lips smiling, jeweled earrings flashing.

Yang Lu is the type of entrepreneur who knew how to ride the wave to success, detecting a need at just the right moment. After having worked for foreign companies for fifteen years, she went out on her own, opening one of the first schools in executive and leadership training in Beijing. In a country as competitive as China, with a high regard for oratory skills and education, she attracted clients immediately. She was very selective about who she would accept as a client, because she cringed at the thought of being compared to one of the self-help gurus whose books fill the shelves of airport bookstores. She only accepted high-level executives of major companies, including the Bank of China, CCTV television network, and investment funds, among others.

It was virtually impossible to talk with her directly. To my frustration, her personal assistant was an impenetrable fortress: "Yang Lu is very tired, she has been in meetings nonstop this week," she would say, when she answered the phone at all. More than once, she told me her boss was in a meeting, only to contradict herself later with a cool, "She's on a business trip and I don't know when she's returning. It would be best if you didn't bother her." I kept trying. After several weeks, mysteriously, it finally paid off.

The offices of Ya Zhi, the name of Yang Lu's company, are located in a skyscraper in the CBD, one of Beijing's business districts. I ran into the first employees in their purple uniforms in the elevator. The women wore suits with purple jackets, silk blouses, hair pulled back tightly and worn in a neat chignon, low heels: an esthetic painstakingly designed by their boss, she herself would explain later.

At the door, a manager greeted me dressed in the same uniform, only a couple of shades darker. At first glance, it was an office like any other, with lines of cubicles filled with employees working away, carpet on the floor, the sound of ringing phones, printers and fax machines. But one thing stood out. It was the music playing in the background. "Is that Tibetan music?" I asked my guide. "Yes, they are Buddhist chants. Professor Yang Lu[2] likes to listen to them while she works," she commented, as she opened her boss's door and ushered me inside her office.

Yang Lu was going through a pile of papers. She stood to shake my hand, but abruptly sneezed. "I'm so sorry, I have a cold," she apologized, and turned away from me to discreetly blow her nose. "My assistant told me you were very interested in talking to me, and I didn't want to cancel our appointment. You'll have to put up with my awful voice right now," she said. Her eyes were puffy, her nose red. The Tibetan chants were louder inside her office. I noticed some sticks of incense burning on a small wooden altar, placed on a shelf among her books on business management. Yang Lu invited me to sit down. She spoke into an intercom, asking for someone to bring us tea, and then sat down on her purple leather sofa, under a portrait of the Buddha.

Why the chants playing in the background? "They help me to focus while I'm working," she explained. "I believe that my employees benefit from listening to them, too." She went on to explain how her office was decorated, a curious hybrid between a temple and a museum of business achievement, which made perfect sense to her. One wall was covered from floor to ceiling with plaques and certificates she had been awarded over the course of her career: an award for being one of the ten best companies in the country, the "Pioneer in Training Business Executives" award, "Member of the Committee on Human Resources in China," "Prize for Brand Marketing." Next to the window hung a brilliantly colored tapestry, representing the Tibetan Wheel of Life.[3] "A friend from Lhasa brought that for me," she explained, softly touching it. On the shelves were mineral crystals, small glass bottles, a golden tiger, and several jade carvings of various animals. She told me she had decided on every detail, from the shade of the walls down to the opacity of the curtains. The name of her company, Ya Zhi (雅致), elegance, had also been her idea.

"In my opinion, elegance, good taste and refinement are qualities that managers and their employees should possess. The color purple evokes romance and rationality, because we have to heed our impulses without falling into sentimentality. A shade of pink would have been too feminine. Purple represents both sexes," she clarified.

Yang Lu could not be more Chinese in her sense of duty, and, as I would discover later, in her sense of humor. But she didn't like talking in circles around a topic, like many of her compatriots did; she'd rather get right to the point. She told me candidly that the biggest burden holding back Chinese countries was the legacy of Confucius, which dictated a very rigid hierarchical structure. To Confucius, the interests of the group come before the interests of the individual, and maintaining cohesion and harmony had to be the top priority before anything else. Yang Lu believed the typical pyramid corporate structure where the bosses give orders and the employees obey fails in the end. "Workers in this country are used to the hierarchy, they're used to obeying without thinking about the consequences their actions will have on other departments, or on the business as a whole," Yang Lu explained to me. She didn't think that harmony and humility would necessarily lead to business success. On the contrary, they could result in complacency and stagnation. When the staff was afraid of taking any initiative for fear of looking like a show-off, they didn't do anything beyond what their job description clearly stipulates.

She served us tea in porcelain cups, and put some medicinal herbs in hers. "I hope I can get over this cold quick. My calendar is packed through the next two months," she sighed. "And I have a hard time delegating. I do just the opposite of what I tell my students to do." To explain her work, she took some folders out of a file drawer filled with articles about her that had been published in many different magazines and newspapers.

When she started Ya Zhi in 2002, executive training was almost nonexistent in the country. The Chinese are used to watching supposed experts on television (some are, in fact, actors) who would share the secrets of their professional success, so they didn't entirely understand why it would be necessary to go take classes to learn how to do better at work. Yang Lu got tired of explaining how her business had nothing to do with those self-help gurus. Luckily, her good contacts gave her their vote of confidence. She hired about a dozen exceptionally successful businesswomen, public relations executives, and psychologists (also all women) to give the seminars, while she oversaw selecting their client base and establishing relationships with companies and institutions. She had been at it for a decade. Hardly a week went by when she didn't have a corporate seminar to introduce, or a guest appearance on a television show.

Although her services were personalized, over time she came to realize that all of her students needed to start with some basics. For example, they needed to learn what the difference was between a group, and a team. "It's not obvious to the Chinese. We ask our students what is the difference between an NBA basketball team and a group of tourists traveling with a tour group, and they have to really think for a while before coming up with an answer." Another of the first lessons trained executives to make business decisions based on professional criteria, and not on personal friendship. "In China, the better the boss likes you, the better he treats you, and vice-versa. It shouldn't be like that," she insisted.

Motivating workers was the hardest part. "Take a look at any company. Whenever the boss is not there, the employees take a break." She was right, at least when it came to office environments. China as a whole has one of the highest rates of worker absenteeism in the world.[4] We both had friends who took naps at work whenever they could, or would lie about having doctors' appointments so they could stay home watching television. Of course, there are also millions of workers who don't take a single day off, ever, because if they do, they won't get paid. They live on automatic pilot, getting out of bed to go to the factory, plant or restaurant. But, as Yang Lu points out, the bosses of those workers don't arrange for motivational courses for their staff.

Many executives called her up, frustrated, because their best employees would quit after only a few months on the job, and move over to the competition. Workplace turnover has diminished somewhat because of the economic crisis in the West, and its repercussions in China, but it is still very high. According to Yang Lu, turnover was a positive thing up to a point, because it meant that the market was moving and there was competition, but it also had consequences. Many executives were aware that something had to change, but they weren't sure what it was.

Yang Lu hadn't gotten to where she was out of vocation. As a little girl, she had dreamed of being a ballerina and a military officer. Her parents were members of the Army, and had instilled a love of music and dance in her. In the early eighties, she attended the Military Academy of the Arts in Beijing, one of the most prestigious institutions in the country. An injury had kept her from enrolling in the Dance department, so she ended up studying technical engineering there. She loved it. It was a unique, exciting time in China, as the country was opening up economically, and the people were starting to recover from the traumas of the Cultural Revolution of 1966–1976.[5] Dressing stylishly or wearing makeup were no longer considered bourgeois affectations; the universities enjoyed unprecedented freedom of expression.[6] Now the party line wasn't about achieving economic equality, it was to get rich. Deng Xiaoping established Special Economic Zones[7] in several cities on the southern coast, virtual teaching laboratories of capitalism to showcase the country's new economic openness and attract investment from the outside world. The first foreign companies began arriving and setting up shop.[8] The Chinese people were bursting with ideas and creative energy, excited to move their country forward. Determined and visionary, Yang Lu felt she had to get on that train. In 1991, as soon as she graduated from the university, she accepted an offer from the French company Bull. Three years later, she moved on to Hewlett Packard, where she spent eight years, a time she looks back on very fondly.

"I learned invaluable lessons at those two jobs. I realized that foreign companies had a big advantage over us. HP had a thirty-year history when I started there, and over that time they had created their own corporate culture. They worked in a different way. At first, it seemed odd to me that my bosses separated their personal lives from their work. They were very responsible at the office, but when the work day was over, or when they were on vacation, they didn't answer their phones. Chinese businesspeople tend to spend twenty-four hours a day working. But they don't know how to be productive." She kept sneezing every few minutes because of her cold, although she never suggested cutting our conversation short.

She served fresh cups of tea. In her opinion, the weak point of China's private companies was their lack of experience. The oldest businesses had been in existence for less than three decades (until 1988, they didn't even legally exist) and they had to learn so many things in a hurry. It went without saying that China had undergone a radical economic transformation in record time, going from Maoism to state-sponsored capitalism. In 1979 the agricultural collectives were dissolved, and each family was allowed to cultivate their own plot of land. For the first time, people were not obligated to live, eat and work together. Instead they could decide for themselves what they wanted to plant, and they could enjoy the fruits of their labor. With this paradigm shift, known as *gaizhi* (改制, transforming the system) tens of thousands of state-owned companies were closed or restructured.[9] Forty-five million jobs disappeared,[10] and many people set off to start their own businesses.

Today forty million companies are registered in China, and of those 93% are private.[11] However—and this is the "quid" of the matter—the State still controls strategic sectors of the economy through their massive petroleum, gas, cement, insurance and telecommunications firms.[12] Eight of every ten members of the board of directors of these companies are appointed directly by the Communist Party. They are less efficient than private companies,[13] but the major banks, also state-owned, extend the most favorable credit terms to them. Many experts wryly observe that, at the end of the day, they are all part of the same big enterprise: "China, Inc."

Yang Lu assumed that independent business owners like herself would be relegated to the minor leagues. Her biggest concerns were securing investors and getting financing, since over 90% of small businesses could not get loans through the big banks.[14] But Chinese business owners are extremely persistent as a rule, and leave no stone unturned, asking friends, family, and especially private lenders for money. This parallel system of credit moves enormous sums: approximately 630 billion dollars per year, the equivalent of almost 10% of China's gross domestic product in 2011.[15]

In some areas, not having access to credit is causing widespread social instability. In Wenzhou, the city that produces the majority of the world's pens and cigarette lighters, almost a hundred businessmen disappeared in 2011,[16] because of the rising cost of raw materials and the shrinking number of orders. But more than anything they went under because they could not pay off the loan sharks, who eventually were charging whopping 70% interest rates. After the sudden massive disappearance of their bosses, thousands of workers couldn't collect paychecks they were owed, and tensions mounted, putting the government on guard. The authorities were aware that loan sharks operated freely with no oversight at all in most parts of the country, and even resorted to kidnapping and torture to get loans repaid. But business owners still had to rely on them as long as they had no other alternative.

Where would China be without the private sector? In areas like Zhejiang, the cradle of entrepreneurship, more than six million small and midsize companies employ most of the workforce. There are many tenacious, sacrificing workers leading the boom, some with incredible stories. You don't have to look hard to come across the typical millionaire who dropped out of school at sixteen, found a loan for 300 yuan (47 dollars) from a cousin to buy two sewing machines, then resold them for a profit of 100 yuan, and with that amount opened his own business, for example a button factory. Now he runs a company with 1,500 employees, and is planning on expanding his operation into distributing clothing, tools or agricultural products. Yang Lu knew many such stories. "Our parents were used to staying in the same company for their entire lives. My generation has had to adapt, and we want more."

Yang Lu didn't understand people used to the "iron rice bowl," a guaranteed job with good benefits.[17] She identifies with people who have risked everything to start their own business, or as the Chinese saying goes, have *xia hai* (下海), "plunged into the sea of business," giving up a steady job in a state-run factory to roll with the waves in the ocean of private enterprise. "We Chinese are do-ers, we're not afraid, we accept the risk and if it goes badly, then we move on to the next thing. Of course we're not all like this. The middle class especially doesn't like pressure. Those who work for foreign companies or hold management positions do tolerate pressure, but the rest are content to just live their lives," she said, signaling with a look of disgust toward her employees through the glass window.

On clear days, Yang Lu can see Jianwai SOHO from her window, a residential complex that symbolizes the success of the private sector. Led by the multimillionaire married couple Pan Shiyi and Zhang Xin, SOHO is the biggest real estate devel-opment company in China. Few couples are as media-friendly: they have won dozens of international awards, they throw lavish parties for the rich and famous, and they have millions of fans on the Internet. Since 1995, they have constructed almost thirty mil-lion square feet of property, and they are in the process of building several more developments.[18]

The Jianwai was their first project, and it was a stunning suc-cess. The twenty white towers designed by the Japanese architect Riken Yamamoto perfectly embodied the functional design that the new upper class yearned for in Maoism's wake. Everyone wanted to buy one of the light-filled residences in those glass tow-ers, all between seven hundred and two-thousand square feet. Three of every four buyers were Chinese younger than thirty-five years old, urbane business owners, many having been educated abroad. Some had bars installed over their windows, because they weren't accustomed to such dramatic views and suffered attacks of vertigo.

Pan Shiyi and Zhang Xin are living proof that many Chinese millionaires start from nothing. Over thirty years, a goat herder can end up behind the wheel of an expensive sports car. Pan grew up in Gansu, one of the poorest provinces, under the stigma of having a counterrevolutionary father. His family had to give up two of his sisters for adoption. He threw himself into his studies and was accepted at a university in Beijing. He worked for the Ministry of Land and Resources, and then resigned that position to go to Shenzhen on the southeast coast and work for a private company. Then he tried his luck on Hainan island, "China's Hawaii," where the housing market was just taking off. Buying, selling, and developing a nose for deals, he became a titan of the sector.

In 1994, Pan Shiyi met Zhang Xin, who had also risen high, climbing up from the very lowest rungs of the socioeconomic ladder. One of Zhang Xin's earliest memories is the metal rice bowl she shared with her classmates at school, at a time when "everything was gray, and everyone dressed the same."[19] At fourteen, she and her mother moved to Hong Kong, which was still a British colony. She worked in a shop during the day, and went to school at night. She worked hard, scrimping and saving until she had enough money to buy a plane ticket to London, and off she went, with little more than a wok and a Chinese-English dictionary under her arm. That trip was a turning point. She loved the museums, the opera and how the British dressed. She earned a scholarship to study for her Master's degree at Cambridge University, and was hired by Goldman Sachs in New York. Then she went back to Beijing, excited by the business opportunities opening up with the economic reforms. She met Pan, and in less than a week, they decided to marry. A year later they founded SOHO.

The couple claims they are apolitical, although they post incisive comments about the government on Weibo, the Chinese version of Twitter. The real estate sector "is so controlled by Government policies, that one spends more time trying to figure out the laws than doing business," Zhang Xin complained to her 2.4 million followers in August 2011. Pan Shiyi is also very active on the Internet. He has criticized the air pollution in Beijing, citing the measurements performed by the United States embassy, much more comprehensive than the Chinese government's own data, and he participates in debates and forums on topics of high interest. When Steve Jobs, the president of Apple died, a very popular brand in China in spite of the scandals involving its subcontractors,[20] Pan wrote on Weibo: "Apple's board should immediately approve the mass production of a new iPhone and iPad that cost less than 1,000 yuan (157 dollars) so that more people could afford them. That would be the best way to commemorate Jobs." One of his followers responded, "If one day the president [of SOHO] Pan Shiyi dies, please, put homes on the market for less than 100 yuan per square foot. Billions of people would commemorate him." The message was resent thousands of times. Still, he is generally well-liked on the Internet, because he takes the criticism with a sense of humor. Some say he tries to be low-key because he suffered so much when his father was persecuted under Maoism. Other more cynical rumors circulating suggest that his hands can't be totally clean since he's so rich and involved in the real estate business, and that's why he doesn't say too much.

I t's hard to measure how connected Chinese business leaders are to the Communist Party (CCCP). It's no secret that the magnates at the helm of the public companies have a direct line with Zhongnanhai, the seat of the central government in Beijing. Some came from high-level positions within the Administration,[21] or aspire to a seat in the Politburo. It is safe to say there is a revolving door between the Government and businesses, exacerbated by rampant nepotism.

In China, political leaders habitually appoint their own children to run state companies. Former Prime Minister Wen Jiabao did this himself in February 2012, when he named his son Wen Yunsong as president of China Satcom, the public satellite giant. According to *The New York Times*, Mr. Wen's relatives have controlled assets worth at least $2.7 billion. His predecessors Li Peng and Zhu Rongji also profited from their positions to influence investments in strategic sectors like energy and telecommunications. Reviewing the lists of high-level managers at the state-run companies one by one, dozens of famous names stand out.[22] The topic is treaded on very lightly in the official media, and criticisms are voiced only indirectly, with the exception of Weibo. On China's version of Twitter, people routinely express their revulsion for endemic nepotism and corruption.

In 2011, the very official *People's Daily* published the results of a survey in which 91% of the respondents believed that all of the wealthy families in China had contacts in the government.

The common workaday folk scream to high heaven when a photo goes around the Internet of one of these privileged scions at a party, surrounded by models, movie stars and elite athletes, or crowing about their achievements on Facebook.

As for private entrepreneurs, the Communist Party has begun courting them, after excluding them from their ranks for years. Then, they were a "symbol of capitalism," but now they are "also the builders of socialism with Chinese characteristics."[23] Private businesspeople want to cultivate a relationship with the Party, a select club that hands out the best business opportunities. The billionaire Li Shufu, chairman of Zhejian Geely Holding Group, China's biggest privately owned car firm which owns Volvo, candidly described the situation in an interview: "It's a relationship between the ruler and the ruled. Chinese business owners have to implement the Party's directives in their work. We do what the Government tells us. It is a fundamental principle of China's economy and market, and there's nothing to discuss. I think it's good that we listen to the Party and follow the Government's instructions."[24]

Now the Party actively seeks the support of these leaders in the private sector, which generates a significant portion of the country's wealth and innovates more than the monolithic state companies, which can execute infrastructure projects efficiently, but are not so good at generating products that add value. If China wants to cast off its image as the world's factory, many experts believe it will have to rely on private industry.

The latest generation of business people have their sights fixed on the innovators in Silicon Valley, not on the Communist Party. In the major cities, project incubators that emulate California's start-ups have come into fashion. In stylishly designed offices, complete with game rooms and complimentary refreshments, twenty-something Chinese hone their ideas as a team, and try to seduce investors to help make their vision a reality. In the event that they do succeed, they fear just two things: one, that a big company like Baidu (the Chinese Google) will steal their idea, taking advantage of China's weak laws protecting intellectual property. And two, that the government will shoot them down.[25]

Whenever she spoke about the Party, Yang Lu measured her words very carefully. She knew that maintaining a good relationship with the powers that be was critical to her survival. And the Government helped her out too, hiring her to give talks to the state companies, and giving her publicity through the official media outlets. She would only venture to criticize the *nou-*

veau riche, aware that some of them were Government function-aries.

"With the development of our economy, many people have made money, but don't know how to spend it. They behave pathetically. If they go shopping for handbags, since the brand Louis Vuitton is familiar to them, they'll buy ten; if they see diamonds, they'll grab a handful, like they're rocks. They're not curious; they don't have their own ideas. They go to a concert and fall asleep. They have no idea who Chopin or Tchaikovsky were. And they don't care. There are too many people in this country, and there are very few who are educated and have good taste."

One of her seminars is aimed at executives with the roughest edges: "How to Appreciate Luxury, and Analyze Investments." She has them read her book *The Banquet of Taste*. She gave me a copy, which comes with a DVD. On the cover, superimposed over her company's unmistakable purple logo is a photo of her, wearing a thick string of pearls, raising a crystal glass. Her favorite chapter expounds upon wine and how to drink it. She got the idea after meeting with some construction managers so coarse she was at her wit's end. "Many Chinese drink wine like hard liquor, emptying their glasses in one swallow," she explained. "They have no idea about all the culture around it."

She did not criticize foreigners, and I wondered if that was out of respect for me. I wanted to know what she thought of business leaders in other parts of the world. As much as she talked about the glamour of the west in her books, I imagined she probably didn't believe they were all so polished and refined. She assured me that in her twenty years of experience, she had worked with geniuses and incompetents alike from many different countries. I pressed her to be a little more specific, and she laughed. "Alright, we always say that you Westerners are lazy."

To Yang Lu, the Chinese people's biggest virtue is their dili-

gence. It is programmed in their DNA: if they took on an assign-
ment, they would see it through to completion even if it meant
staying up all night for several days in a row. She was fascinated by
cultural differences that arose when it came time to do business.
She understood the frustration foreigners felt when faced with a
lack of professionalism on the part of some of her compatriots.
And she empathized with her countrymen's frustrations when
they had to deal with a particularly pretentious Westerner. She
understood why Westerners liked to spell everything out in writing, while the Chinese rarely said "no" to anything directly, and
placed much less importance on a signed piece of paper. A foreigner could consider in advance whether the project made sense
or not. They didn't blindly follow orders, but they were less disci-
plined. Many arrived in China with a full agenda of meetings and
gifts for their potential local business partners, assuming they
could make a deal over a dinner. Days later, getting on the plane
back home, they had no idea exactly where their negotiations had
left off. With a keen understanding of both worlds, Yang Lu explained to her students that time and contacts do not carry the
same weight in both cultures. The Chinese need to forge a personal relationship first, and they don't mind spending hours and
hours with their guests; while an American or European can lose
their patience when their hosts invite them to spend the afternoon
at the local museum, and later treat them to a lavish fifteen-course
dinner, and take them to a karaoke bar after that. Westerners self-
promote and unabashedly talk about their own accomplishments,
while to the Chinese this is seen as egotistical and childish. They
are more comfortable with self-criticism, not because they do not
care what others think of them, but because they are obsessed with
what kind of image they project. That is why they will never forgive someone who makes a fool of them. Yang Lu uses specific
examples of these different modes of behavior in her classes.

Thanks to her talent for relating to people and her ability to put in very long days, she was a sought-after guest at parties and on television shows. And a guaranteed success. Her day could start with an early morning conference presentation at the university, followed by breakfast with a client; then her driver may take her to give a seminar for business executives or speak at another conference, and on many afternoons she would go on from there to a television studio for an interview. Usually she would have accepted a dinner invitation in the evening. Sometimes her work demanded that she spend fifteen hours in heels, ever-mindful of the body language she projected, maintaining her sharp mental focus. Her keen intellect and sharp wit, but with a very human touch made her stand out from the other celebrities competing for space in the media.

Yang Lu is an inspiration for Chinese women between forty and sixty years old, a kind of Oprah Winfrey, as my friend Xing[26] put it. Xing's mother seemed to be among her die-hard fans, with copies of Yang Lu's books *The Banquet of Taste, Develop Your Charisma*, and others on her nightstand. To female television viewers, she is mesmerizing to watch, from the first minute she appears on the screen. My friend, who wasn't yet twenty-five, was dying to meet her and begged me to introduce her.

She warmly received us in her office, wearing a black suit with a tangerine jacket. Always expert at public relations, Yang Lu immediately gave Xing several books, and asked her some friendly questions to break the ice. Observing how extremely respectfully my friend answered her, it struck me that Yang Lu really was an icon in China. "My mother reads every article you write in the women's magazines. She's not a business person, but she really admires you," Xing stammered. Yang Lu responded smoothly, she was used to the accolades. She asked Xing what her mother's name was, and personally autographed one of the books for her.

"Please tell your mother I thank her for her interest," she said politely.

Xing lowered her gaze. "You know, my mother really likes how you talk about the importance of establishing your own independence, because she's getting separated, she needs to rebuild her life. I can tell she's really depressed, and that's also why I wanted to meet you, I thought maybe you could give me some advice that could help her," the words rushed out. There was an uncomfortable silence. The Xing I knew was very reserved, she had never told me she was worried about her mother.

Yang Lu furrowed her brow, and for a minute I feared she regretted having agreed to the meeting. She let out a long sigh, and pulled at the sleeves of her jacket. "You're not the first person to tell me this. Chinese society restricts women, and doesn't let them grow. We're always told what we have to do. When we're little girls, our fathers choose the school we will attend; when we get older, the boys come around, and often the one we like doesn't like us back. Then we get married, have a baby, and suddenly we're mothers. We have to devote ourselves to our family, to our babies and husbands. All our energy goes into our home." She called her secretary through the intercom and asked her to bring us some refreshments, and she settled herself on the couch. This was going to take a while.

Xing seemed relieved, and she ventured to tell us the whole story, from the beginning. A few months ago, her mother had found out that her husband was cheating on her. This came as no surprise. It seemed they had never gotten along, and they talked about it openly. But she was devastated to learn he didn't even want to keep up appearances anymore. "My father has a younger girlfriend. He went off to live with her, and now all the neighbors know they're separated. All day long my mother says she's worthless, that she has no life. She would have preferred that he had stayed at home, and they had agreed to some kind of arrange-ment," Xing explained. "Don't say that," Yang Lu replied. It seemed like a scene from a soap opera, they were both so sincere. "Many women in this country have no self-esteem. They're not independent. When they find out their husbands are cheating on them, they're already fifty years old, and they don't know what to do with themselves."

She remembered a conference she had given about women and self-esteem, and she put the DVD in the player. "I'm going to give this to you so you can bring it to your mother," she said to Xing. It was a two-hour video, but she fast-forwarded to the end, where she interviewed several businesswomen. "These testimonials are very interesting, maybe they will be inspiring to your mother. Right now she's very angry, she doesn't know what her place is. I know many women who have gone through the same thing. They put all of their time and energy into their family, they stop work-ing, and when their marriages end, they see it was a trap. They can't turn to their parents for comfort because they're old, or to their children, so as not to worry them."

She explained that over the course of her career, she had worked hard to avoid having certain labels put on her. She studied engineering, and worked for years surrounded by men, in envi-ronments where all women did was serve tea. For all the lip ser-vice Maoism paid to gender equality, women's emancipation had yet to arrive in China. To start up her own business, Yang Lu had sacrificed money and time. She had plunged into the sea of busi-ness. And now, at forty-one, she was going to take a little break, for the first time since she had begun working. She took a sip of tea, and announced she was three months' pregnant.

W e didn't meet again until after she had given birth. She had twins, a boy and a girl. Six months later, Yang Lu resumed her frenetic schedule of conferences, debates, seminars in her company's purple headquarters, smiles trained on television cameras. A bigger star than ever, she launched Yadro, the first business coaching portal for professional women. She uploaded videos of her classes onto the Internet. She partnered with a South Korean designer friend and created her own line of women's clothing, which she modeled herself for the pages of the catalog. Hundreds of business titans, government officials and star-struck students attended the first fashion show unveiling the line. "Have you seen *Titanic?*" she asked, toying with her necklace, flashing a winning smile. "These are the same jewels that were in the movie."

6

✦✦✦✦

Living Underground

They are called rats, and they have become a symbol of Beijing's red-hot real estate market. Because of soaring housing costs, there are at least a million people living underground, only able to afford a rented room in the basements of skyscrapers or converted bomb shelters in their nation's capital. Obsessed with the possibility of a Soviet nuclear attack, in 1969 President Mao Zedong ordered the construction of underground shelters that would stretch for eighteen miles beneath the city, able to accommodate half of the population if war ever broke out. The subterranean city center was rife with holes from all the tunneling, like a giant Swiss cheese. A half-century after their construction began, parts of this underground city have been converted into living quarters. This is the only housing option for many students, waiters, hairdressers, office workers, the newly divorced starting their lives over, and many others trying to eke out a living.

Chen Erfei, thirty years old, arrived in the capital in 2009 from a village in the middle of the country where indoor plumbing was considered a luxury. He works as a security guard in a residential complex for upper-class Chinese and foreigners, in a trendy neighborhood filled with fashionable bars and clubs. When his workday ends, he spends the night in a subbasement with three hundred other people. Beds cost sixty-five dollars a month, four times less than renting a room above ground. Chen does not have to pay, because his company provides these barracks-like rooms to sleep for its workers.

He is a *mingong*, a worker who migrated from the countryside to the city. There are almost three hundred million Chinese in this situation, most younger than thirty, and in Beijing they make up a third of the city's twenty million inhabitants. China's economic miracle would not have been possible without the extreme sacrifices they make, leaving their families behind to keep the factories afloat, construct high-rise buildings, clean offices, and serve meals in restaurants. They send almost all of their earnings home, and, if they're lucky, they manage to go visit their families once a year, with suitcases stuffed with gifts. Their small children often don't recognize them.

Chen is proud of where he lives. To get to his room, he enters a skyscraper's lobby, goes down a stairwell and walks past the boiler room, the machines there roaring at deafening levels. At the end of the hall, a set of doors open onto the parking garage and bicycle racks. Past the garage is the bomb shelter, now converted into dozens of rooms. The first time he took me there, four sickly looking boys wearing doorman uniforms lay sleeping beside the bathrooms. As we approached they snapped awake and stood up, mumbling a greeting, staring down at the floor. They couldn't have been more than seventeen years old. "They just got here," Chen said briskly. An old-timer sat beside them, although he was just as frail, and had to roll his pants down over the top of his belt.

Chen talks very softly, with a Henan accent, substituting the n's for l's. Every once in a while his voice breaks, as if he were in the throes of adolescence and it was still changing. He wears his hair in a short buzz cut, and has a suntanned complexion, a long, slender neck, and very white teeth, especially for someone who has never been able to afford to visit a dentist. He gestures slowly with his hands, and stares off into space. He has such a delicate physique and mannerisms, one imagines him composing poetry in his room. But nothing could be further from the reality.

He shares a room with seven coworkers, all security guards for the same development. There were four narrow metal bed frames squeezed into a space of one-hundred-thirty square feet. Pieces of plywood rested atop the bed frames with thin cotton-filled bedrolls over them, some of them too short—Chen told me his feet dangled over the edge as he slept. There were no pictures on the walls, no rug, no windows to let any daylight find its way into their underground world. Two of the beds were occupied: a boy with terrible acne leaned on his elbows and played a game on his phone, while another was curled up in the fetal position, snoring. "After work, we're so tired all we want to do is sleep," Chen explained.

On the floor were several plastic containers, mismatched shoes, a stool, and dust bunnies the size of a fist. Someone had left a bowl of half-eaten instant noodle soup. The room smelled of sweat and food.

"What's it like living here?" I asked.

"I can't complain," Chen smiled.

When he thought about what his life would have been like if he had stayed in his village, he explained, he felt fortunate.

I n 1981, when Chen was born, China had begun to open up its economy,[1] but in the Chengjia Valley, at the Yellow River basin, nothing had noticeably changed. Among the two thousand residents of the village, a tiny community by Chinese standards, Chen's family was in an enviable position, because his father worked for a state factory and had a steady paycheck he could count on at the end of every month. His mother taught in a nearby school. A plot of land to farm and a pen with pigs and chickens guaranteed they would have food to put on the table.

Chen remembers they were among the first households to have a television. "The neighbors would come over at night to watch the revolutionary soap operas. And we had a radio and a washing machine. We were very lucky because we had a worker in the family." And his parents cultivated their land, which meant Chen and his two brothers had to wake up bright and early. His grandmother took care of them and his cousins. She had eight grandchildren to look after in all. "Since she didn't know which kid to deal with first, in the end she didn't deal with any of us," Chen joked. He doesn't remember ever confiding in anyone in his family. "In the villages in the countryside, people don't talk much, they are not used to expressing their feelings, not even with their own children. A few times in the evening, my mother apologized for not being able to spend time with us. She reminded us we were the envy of the village because we had a television."

The biggest concern parents had was to marry off their offspring as soon as possible, and to accomplish this, each son had to have his own place to live. "Without a house, in the village you're a nobody," Chen states. "Young men spend years building their home, and when they finish they feel like they've achieved success." When he finished secondary school at seventeen, his family wasn't so enviable anymore, because his father had lost his job at the factory. Many state-owned industries were being dismantled at that time, and twenty million people found themselves[2] suddenly unemployed. His mother could not save enough money on her own to pay for the bride prices and homes for her sons, so Chen had to go out and find a job. First he worked washing dishes in a hotel kitchen. Then he enlisted in the Army, until a relative who had a printing press in Shaanxi, the neighboring province, called and offered him a job. He worked there for a few months, but his relative paid him very poorly, because he was "family", and Chen could barely save any money. Not a day went by when his mother or grandmother didn't call him and pointedly remind him that he had to find a wife. "They told me, if you don't know anybody, we'll find a woman for you ourselves. There are girls around here who would do just fine," he remembers. Tired of all the pressure, he went back to his village to find himself a wife.

C hen confesses that he never imagined doing anything else with his life. His mission was to build himself a house, get married, and have a child, a son, if possible. That is what he had been taught, following Confucian tradition. At twenty-four he was behind schedule, as most of his friends and cousins had settled down already.

All of the romanticism the Chinese love to see at the movies is completely absent from real life. With few exceptions, marriage is like a contract two individuals enter into to pool their resources and earnings. They call it *guorizi* (过日子), "passing the days," to be together simply because life is easier when one has a partner. No more sentimental than that.

Chen had known Zhao Li since high school. They had talked a lot in class and got along well. When his parents began badgering him to find a wife, it occurred to him that it could be her. They had talked on the phone a few times, and he had taken her for rides on the back of his motorbike in the summer, racing through the fields, feeling the wind on their faces. That was all, but for Chen, it was enough.

"I don't remember how I told her how I felt about her." He

scratches his head with his tan, rough fingers, trying to remember. "Now teenagers watch television and they learn about those kinds of things from the shows, but back then we didn't have anything to learn from. I think that one day I just told her I wanted to introduce her to my parents. She was quiet for a minute, and then she said yes. That formalized our relationship. Right then we knew we were going to get married."

Their families didn't make it easy. As tradition dictates, Chen's parents went over to meet Zhao's parents at her house, and the mutual interrogation began: how many male children are there in your family? How many own their own homes? And plots of land? Does your son intend to include some livestock in the bride price? Are you sure your daughter could get pregnant quickly? Do any diseases run in your family? And both sides hedged their bets. "My parents introduced me to two other girls, and Zhao Li's family did the same because they didn't think I would manage to have our house built before the wedding," Chen recalls.

Finally an agreement was reached, and they settled on a price. Before the wedding, Chen gave his prospective in-laws 8,880[3] yuan ($1,400) as a bride price and a deposit of 20,000 yuan ($3,200), which would be returned to him once the house had been constructed. Until then, the couple would live with Chen's parents. "I hated my in-laws for making me pay so much money up front," he remembers, frowning. "But over time they have been very nice to me, and I understand that every family has to take care of their own. Getting married is like closing a deal, you can't take it lightly."

The wedding was a major event for the village. For years Chen's parents had had to put up with speculation from the neighbors about their son, who at twenty-four had never had a girlfriend, and they wanted to celebrate his marriage in as high a style as possible. It all followed local custom. The day before the wedding, the bridegroom's house filled up with women cooking and men coming and going with chickens, pigs, sacks of rice and vegetables, boxes of firecrackers, cigarettes, and rice liquor. Chen and his cousins rented sixty round tables that each sat eight people, and managed to set them up between the house and the garden. They hung up images of the Chinese character traditionally associated with weddings: "double happiness," 囍 (*shuangxi*), on red die-cut paper. Then they went to find the bride.

A caravan of ten cars filled with the bridegroom's friends and cousins pulled up at Zhao Li's house. Her parents served everyone noodles. Then, as Chen tells it, a kind of fictional battle ensued between his side, who wanted to "kidnap" the bride, and Zhao Li's relatives, who had to "protect" her and keep her from leaving the house. The bridegroom's mission was to find and go to his future wife, but first he had to pass a series of tests. And that was the funny part. First, they made him show his respect to her family.

"Zhao Li's friend kept shouting at me, laughing hard: Now bow down eight times before her mother's brothers! Now bow to her oldest cousin! Again, you didn't bow low enough!" Chen says. He remembers getting a sharp pain in his lower back after bowing down to her grandmother so many times. "Before I could pass through the last door to get to the bride's room, they made me do thirty-six bows in a row," he says with a chuckle, rubbing his stomach. "When I could finally get Zhao Li out of her room, I had to give a red envelope[4] with money in it to each of her cousins and siblings. If I hadn't, they wouldn't have let us get in the car."

Together they arrived at the banquet at Chen's parents' house, which was open all day so that the whole village could come by and raise a glass. The tables were covered with red table cloths, the color of marriage. They served all the traditional dishes for the occasion: dumplings filled with lotus root, symbolizing fertility; chicken feet, which resemble the feet of a phoenix (the mythological animal symbolizing woman), and lobster, which symbolizes the man, because in Chinese they call it "dragon prawn", and the dragon is masculine. There was plenty of fish, which sounds similar to "abundance," to express to the couple the wish that they would not want for anything. Chen's mother and her sisters bustled back and forth between the stoves and the guests' tables all evening. The family's reputation in the village and their prospects for marrying off their other sons depended on how the wedding went off.

The wedding night wasn't exactly intimate. According to local custom, friends and family of the bridegroom would go to pester the newlyweds, so the first night Chen and Zhao Li officially spent the night together, a group of drunk wedding guests burst into the bedroom. "We played cards all night. I hadn't eaten anything all day because I was so nervous, and at least with them I could fill my stomach and drink as much as I wanted," he remembers. They ended up getting very drunk. Chen accompanied each of his guests home as Chinese etiquette mandates, and then stumbled back to his house. "I collapsed into bed, and felt how all the pressure of the last few months evaporated. I remember I said to Zhao Li, at last, we're married. Now they'll leave us alone."

When I ask him what he likes about his wife the most, he thinks for a moment and lights up another cigarette. "The best thing is that she gets along so well with my family. Because pretty she's not." That is quintessential Chinese sincerity: they will avoid telling you 'no' directly at almost any cost, but it is perfectly natural for them to point out that you have dark circles under your eyes, or that you shouldn't eat so much because you're getting fat.

We're sitting on a bench in front of the residential complex where he works. On the top floor, next to the television satellite dishes, four brightly lit characters announce the name of the development: Yang Guang Du Shi, or Sun City. He always wants to meet there, because he doesn't know anywhere else. In the three years he's been in Beijing, he has not been to the Forbidden City, or the Temple of Heaven, packed with visitors every day of the year. The boundaries of his world begin at the sentry box where he spends the night shift, and extend to the cybercafé on the same street. Within those parameters are the benches out front, the supermarket on the corner, and a few restaurants, encompassing about two blocks within a city covering six thousand square miles. That has been his universe since he arrived in the capital.

Once they were married, Chen and Zhao Li moved in with his parents until construction on their house was completed. Those were very happy months, during which they built many pieces of furniture by hand to bring to their new home. Zhao Li opened up a store selling cosmetics and beauty aids in town, and Chen landed a job working for the South-North Water Transfer Project.[5]

But social pressures were building once again. "I don't know what it's like in your country," Chen says, "but here you're supposed to have a baby as soon as possible after the wedding, to avoid setting off a family drama." In China, once again going back to Confucian tradition, the individual must meet certain moral obligations, such as taking care of and obeying one's elders, and ensuring they have a line of descendants. What the individual wants to do with their own life is not relevant.

The couple carried out the task in less than a year. Chen remembers the day they had the baby in detail. "I was working, and my mother called me. She said that Zhao Li was in labor, and that they had taken her to the hospital. I asked my boss if I could leave. I didn't even change my clothes, I got on my motorbike in my work uniform and hit the gas. My heart was beating really hard, so hard." This is the first time he's ever gotten emotional in front of me. He's not speaking in a whisper anymore, he's a proud father. "I thought about my own father when they told him I had been born. He had to go straight from work too, but on a bicycle, pedaling as hard as he could for hours," he explains, as he grips imaginary handlebars and imitates his father's efforts.

When Chen got to the hospital, a typical medical center in rural China where smoking is even permitted in the operating rooms, Zhao Li was still in labor, which went on for several more hours. Chen paced in circles, smoking all the cigarettes he had. Suddenly, he heard a cry that sounded like a cat meowing. A nurse brought him a tiny baby wrapped up in a blanket, the head covered in hair and blood. It wasn't a boy, as the grandparents would have wanted,[6] but for Chen it was the happiest day of his life.

"I looked down at her for a while. I can't describe what I felt, but it was very strong, my stomach hurt, and I was very happy," he exclaims. They named her Ya Zhuo, "elegant girl."

His wife closed her shop so she could take care of their daughter. Chen invested all of their savings into buying a truck. As a driver, he would earn less, but he could spend more time at home, and tend the garden on their little plot of land. They went on for two years like that, until the birth of their second daughter, Xianghan, which made them very happy but depleted their savings even more. At night, Zhao Li sewed silk slippers, but there still wasn't enough money. The family began to pressure Chen to find a job away from the village. "My in-laws and my parents were always telling me, go to Beijing, go to Beijing, that would be the best thing to do."

"Didn't it make them sad to think of you so far away, knowing you'd probably come back to visit once a year at the most?"

"Sad? Not at all, that's what they wanted," he replied, as if it were perfectly normal. After all, in Henan one of every five residents migrate. And he repeats a phrase that seems like the mantra of Chinese migrants: "There wasn't anything to do in the village."

He went one February morning. He wouldn't let Zhao Li accompany him to the train station, since that would have made him even sadder. He hugged his still-sleeping daughters, and carrying a plastic suitcase stuffed with all of his clothes, he left.

The train ride to Beijing was twelve hours long. Chen remembers it like it was yesterday. He didn't want to spend a single yuan more than he had to, so he bought the cheapest ticket, for a hard wooden seat. The aisles were jammed with people talking, sleeping, eating sunflower seeds and chain-smoking. The trains in China are always overbooked. To guarantee yourself a place to sit down, you have to buy a spot in a sleeping car, a narrow pull-down bed, soft or hard, depending on the price. The seats fill up as people arrive, but they keep on selling tickets in the station. It's not unusual to see people crawling through the windows into the train, when it seems like not one more person could possibly fit.

Chen settled himself between a large man, sleeping with his shirt unbuttoned, exposing his ample belly, and a mother who was peeling oranges for her child, throwing the rinds onto the floor. "I tried to visualize what I would do once I got there, so I wouldn't get lost," he said. He had never been in such a large city. The furthest he had ever been from home was in Xi'an, one of the ancient Chinese capitals,[7] twenty times smaller than Beijing.

The train rattled along the tracks as night fell. The expanses of rust-brown fields began to fade away. "I'll never forget the smell. A fat woman went up and down the aisles with food. She was selling soy milk and *mantou*, steamed bread balls. When she got to the end of my car, she took the lids off the round bamboo containers. The air filled with steam, and the guy next to me woke up," Chen remembers. The smell of the bread buns made his mouth water, but they were too expensive. Like most of the other passengers, Chen had brought along a package of instant noodles. He poured boiling water over them, and squatted down to eat along with everyone else.

The only lead he had for landing a job was an ad he had come across a few days earlier in the local paper. The temporary employment agency Xilu offered work for drivers, guards, clerical staff, and stock boys. A steady job, the ad promised. Chen trusted the ad's claim implicitly, since it had a picture of Jackie Chan. The actor, businessman and philanthropist from Hong Kong was a real star in China, and aside from appearing in martial arts movies, he had been featured in antipiracy campaigns in Beijing. He is a controversial figure,[8] but to Chen he personified the ideal of the self-made man.

At dawn the train pulled into Beijing's East Station, which until recently had been the largest train station in Asia. (In 2010 it was overtaken by Shanghai's new Hongqiao Station.) Every day, thousands of migrants from the countryside arrive there, ready to take on the world. They are easy prey for scammers, who pounce on them as soon as they get off the train, promising jobs in exchange for a commission. Some new arrivals eagerly hand over a large part of their savings, confident they will earn it back and more once they start their new jobs, but once they realize they've been had, the con men are nowhere to be found. Some organized crime syndicates place ads in local newspapers, recruiting migrants in their home towns. Once they get to Beijing they are given jobs and get to work, unaware that they will never actually be paid for their labor. Once they figure it out, the workers have been on the job slaving away for a month or more, they have no money to get home, and they are too ashamed to ask their families for help, for fear of being the laughing stock of their villages. Many wander through the train station, asking passersby for money for a train ticket home. Seeing no other option, some commit suicide.

Chen was lucky. He ignored the aggressive offers of cheap

lodging and jobs at the train station. With his Jackie Chan adver-
tisement in his pocket, he got on the metro, and then took a bus to
get to Xilu. Bright new horizons awaited him there, Chan had
promised.

The company painted a very different picture. They only
needed drivers, and they had to know their way around the city.
Unsurprisingly, he did not pass the test. Seeing how disappointed
he was, the staff told him about an industrial park on the outskirts of the city that might be hiring stock boys or security
guards. "I went there, but room and board were not included, and
the salary was so low I didn't think it was worth it, since I
wouldn't have been able to send any money home. So I got on the
metro again and went back downtown." He went into dozens of
restaurants, asking if they were hiring. Then the sun set, and he
noticed how much colder it was at night in Beijing compared to
his village.

He decided to find a cybercafé where he could connect to the
Internet and call his family. As he walked by a residential development, he overheard some security guards joking around in the
little guard booth at the entrance. "I could tell by their accent that
they weren't from Beijing, and I asked them how they had gotten
jobs there," he explains. As it happened, the company was hiring.
"When they told me a room and meals were included, I didn't
think twice." That very night he started working. And sleeping
underground.

He gradually got acclimated to his new home beneath the surface. It was like being in the army again, with the jokes
about women, a constant smell of feet, and the camaraderie of his
peers to stave off loneliness. The lack of privacy did not bother
him, since growing up he had always slept in the same room with
his parents, brothers and grandmother. "The only thing that both-

ered me was the lack of ventilation. The air was so thick and stale, a lot of nights I couldn't sleep."

Security guard shifts are much less grueling than the factory jobs. He has friends who went to work in the factories in Shenzhen, on the southeast coast, instead of migrating to Beijing. Most of their wages are from putting in overtime, in shifts that can stretch through the night. In the summer, when the factories gear up to meet orders for Christmas from the West, the pace is frenetic. Some weeks, his friends only get four or five hours off per day, the bare minimum required to keep them from literally collapsing at their work stations. Chen works a maximum of twelve hours a day, six days a week at his security guard job. The worst part, as he tells it, is working in the winter, when temperatures can plunge to five degrees Fahrenheit. With their navy blue knit caps pulled down low, the guards' hands go numb as they grip their walkie-talkies and thermoses full of tea.

It's very common to eat lunch and dinner out at local restaurants in China. During Mao's reign, the kitchens were communal, and many families only had a hot plate at home. Chen prefers to save his money, and eats his meals in the cafeteria in the basement. He took me there once, and we got in line with our bowls and chopsticks as two pudgy women spooned food out of two huge plastic bins. For breakfast there was tea and *zhou*, a kind of rice porridge and a thick broth which is a staple in the north. For lunch and dinner, the offerings usually include white rice, noodles in clear broth, vegetables sautéed with garlic, chicken and, once in a while, a stew with calves' intestines. We both agreed that almost everything tasted the same.

Chen gets to know his fellow basement dwellers in the cafeteria and when he does his laundry. A cleaning lady, an electrician, or a worker who repairs the water mains could all gather around the same table for lunch. "The first two questions are always, 'where are you from'? And 'how long ago did you leave your village'?" Chen remarks. The girls who work in the hair salon in building three are the only ones who eat separately, keeping to themselves and not talking to anybody else. "They say those girls do something more than just give massages," he murmurs, blushing.

He has one day off a week, and he uses the free time to do laundry, buy something to eat in his room, and play computer games. Thanks to all the migrant workers, the neighborhood cybercafé is always packed. For a few yuan, Chen spends hours playing *Meng San Guo* ('Dream of the Three Ancient Kingdoms'), a battle game based on a classic work of Chinese fiction, *The Romance of the Three Kingdoms*, written six hundred years ago. For the same amount of money, he could get on the bus and explore the city, go to the park, and enjoy some skewered beef and a beer at a sidewalk café. But he says he doesn't feel like it, because time seems to pass more quickly in front of the computer screen.

The happiest time of year for Chinese migrants is the lunar New Year. It falls between January and February,[9] and is the equivalent of Christmas in the West. Families get together, eat as much as they can, and exchange gifts. For the *mingong*, it is the only week of the whole year they spend with their loved ones, and they criss-cross the country in what is considered the greatest annual migration in the world.[10] Train stations are jammed, tickets sell out, and scalpers do a brisk business.

Sometimes migrants cannot return home at all, because they can't get the time off from work, or they haven't saved up enough money to afford a train ticket. That's what happened to Chen his first year away. He was making 900 yuan ($140) a month at the time, and he had hardly saved anything. As his neighborhood was decorated with colorful garlands and paper lanterns for the holiday, he felt a stab of emotion, but it quickly passed. He and a few buddies pooled their money to buy firecrackers, the New Year tradition that the Chinese enjoy the most. They spent hours lighting off strings of them and listening to the crackling explosions until their heads pounded from all the noise. "We drank a lot of rice liquor, and ended up arm-in-arm, singing revolutionary songs," he remembers. The sidewalk was covered with red casings and dust, like streets everywhere throughout China at the New Year.

"There was just one really hard part, when I called home and they handed the phone to Ya Zhuo," he says soberly. His eldest daughter was now old enough to ask him where he was, and when he would be coming home.

Over two years have passed since he first arrived in Beijing, and now Chen is a seasoned veteran. He earns 2,500 yuan, almost three times what he made when he started. He has been given two raises, thanks to the migrant worker strikes that took place in several provinces across the country.[11] He still sends his wages home, but now he occasionally treats himself to a soft drink. From the block of buildings that comprises his world, he has seen changes. "There are many more cars, and the real estate market is through the roof." The residents of Sun City, his only reference point aside from his fellow basement dwellers, drive more SUVs than before. Real estate agents that work in the neighborhood say that apartments in the area are worth twice what they were just five years ago.

Living in Beijing, at least in the small section that he knows, is not bad, Chen says. The hardest part is that his daughters barely recognize him. "They see me once a year. The first time I went home for the holiday, the little one didn't even know who I was. It's normal, since I left when she was barely two months old, but when I picked her up, she wouldn't stop crying until I gave her back to my wife. You can't imagine how much that hurts." On his cell phone he has a video of Ya Zhuo, his oldest, that he recorded a few days before he left. She had just learned to walk, and was babbling away. Chen plays it and smiles broadly, even after having seen it thousands of times it still melts his heart. Ya Zhuo wears a little blue skirt, a pink jacket, and flowers in her pigtails. She clutches a ribbon like the ones used in rhythmic gymnastics in her hand, shaking it up and down, laughing. The video is not the best quality, and her face can't be seen clearly, and it only lasts for around thirty seconds, but still it is Chen's most prized possession. He admits that sometimes watching it makes him cry.

A few months after Chen first began sharing his story with me, he called to let me know that his wife, Zhao Li, had just arrived in Beijing, and had found a job as a cashier in a neighborhood supermarket. The girls were old enough to leave with their grandmother, and with both of them working they could save more money. They were not considering finding an apartment to rent above ground. Like so many couples do, they moved into a little room in the basement of the Sun City residential complex.

Now they're both "rats." Their new home measures eighty-six square feet, and has a bed that doubles as a sofa, and a small table, where they have placed a picture of their daughters. Chen can eat at the cafeteria because he works in the development, but Zhao Li can't. So when she gets home from work, she fixes herself something cold to eat, or buys instant noodles and boils water for them in the bathroom. On her days off, she plays card games on the computer, and talks on the phone with her daughters. "She cries so hard when she watches videos of them," Chen sighs.

Living and working in Beijing while their daughters are raised by their grandparents is the couple's biggest challenge. Without a residency permit,[12] the girls do not have the right to go to school in Beijing. They could only attend a school for migrant children, which are often clandestine, with substandard facilities and a much lower academic standard, or they could make a donation to a public school, literally handing over an envelope with cash, and pay much higher matriculation fees. The public schools' strategy is to prevent children from the countryside from hurting their reputation by weeding them out beforehand with exorbitant charges they cannot afford to pay.

Children of internal migrants have so few alternatives in the city, their parents are forced to leave them behind in their villages. They become *liushou ertong* (留守儿童), "the children left behind." Sociologists consider the phenomenon a serious national problem. There are fifty-eight million children growing up without their parents,[13] and this comes at a very high price to Chinese society. In some parts of Sichuan, Henan and Anhui, all provinces with high poverty rates and high levels of internal migration, eight of every ten children only see their parents once a year.[14] They grow up like wildflowers, without their parents' support, in the care of their grandparents or other relatives. They feel abandoned, and some develop anxiety and self-esteem issues, and depression. Without being closely watched, some have been victims of sexual abuse by their neighbors.

In 2007, several Chinese media outlets published letters that some children of migrants had written to their parents. One of these letters read:

"I was playing in the street, and I saw my mother walking to the bus stop. She was going. She started to walk faster so I wouldn't notice, but I saw her. I ran up to her and held her hand tight. My grandmother separated us so she could get on the bus. I broke free and grabbed on to my mother's clothes, but then my uncle separated us. I started kicking, but when my uncle let me go the bus had already driven away. I was only thinking about bringing my mother back, but the bus was getting smaller and smaller, until it disappeared. I collapsed on the road and cried and cried. The sky was gray, as if I were making it sad. I was so angry, I saw a frog hopping across the road and I kicked it."

Every day, Chen and Zhao Li wonder if leaving their daughters behind will cause them problems in the long run. If they want to save up some money, they have no other choice but to stay in Beijing for a while. Their plan is to eventually go back to their village and open their own business, although they don't know exactly what it will be. The one thing they are both sure of is they don't like Beijing. "Here people look down their noses at us. On the metro, they move away from us like we smell bad," Chen complains. He has seen China's classism at work many times. The same people who hire *mingong* to repair a light fixture or take care of their children talk about them disparagingly. A 2010 study by the Chinese Academy of Social Sciences found that one of every three crimes in the country was committed by a migrant worker born after 1980 (a demographic of approximately one hundred million people). The study pointed to the "social exclusion, the political and economic injustices,[15] the culture shock and the lack of social security" that migrants experience as the root cause of criminal behavior, even more than poverty and low levels of education.

The reality is that without a *hukou*, a residency permit for Beijing, Chen will never be able to claim the rights of a full-fledged citizen. He knows he will be extremely vulnerable, unable to take time off for vacation, or even take sick days. As the cost of living continues to rise, he wonders if being so far away from home is worth it. Many migrants his age share his outlook. Their parents endured all manner of hardships in the cities, because the only other alternative they had was going back to their villages, hard-hit by famine. But Chen's generation are connected to the Internet, and they know what workers in other parts of the country earn. Chen doesn't speculate about what might happen if the Government legalizes labor unions, or abolishes the legal restrictions placed on internal migrants. He does know for sure that he will go wherever the pay is highest. Effects of the one-child policy can be felt in the labor market, as there is no longer a glut of workers, and some factories are offering improved working conditions to attract migrants.

For now, Chen and Zhao Li take it one day at a time. And they have a plan: as soon as they have saved enough money, they'll go back to their village. "This isn't for us," Chen remarks, looking up at the high-rise buildings he keeps watch over for twelve hours a day.

7

✦✦✦✦

China 2.0

She says she's an information junkie, but she doesn't read newspapers or watch television because they're boring. For Ma Chengcheng, twenty-four, the official Chinese media have nothing to offer beyond mind-numbing propaganda. She prefers the Internet. The first thing she does after her alarm goes off at six in the morning is reach for her glasses and laptop on the night table. She greets her 455 Internet friends without even getting out of bed.

"Good morning, I'm here!" she types on her Weibo profile, China's version of Twitter.

In her virtual world, the first half-hour of the day is the most intense. She checks the current weather conditions in Beijing, and posts it. She visits her favorite blogs, and decides what she's going to wear that day, using a computer app designed to help coordinate outfits and accessories.

It takes her almost an hour to get to her office on the bus, and she uses the time to surf the Web on her mobile phone, always following the same routine. First, she updates her status on Weibo and Ren Ren, one of the many local Facebook copycat sites. Then she checks in on her favorite celebrities on Weibo: the actress Yao Chen, the most popular with almost sixteen million followers, and He Jiong, a television host and actor with twelve million followers. The social networking sites pay stars astronomical sums just to maintain an official profile with them, because they know they will attract millions of young people.

She spends the rest of her time looking at the clothes on Taobao, a Web site that has revolutionized e-commerce in China. Inspired by eBay and launched in 2003, it has more than 370 million registered users, and is one of the top twenty most-visited Web sites in the world.[1] Taobao has it all, from vintage vinyl records to the latest home soymilk machine (a very popular item). Regular customers know that they need to be careful, since fakes are mixed in with real brand-name merchandise (the knock-offs are generally not hard to spot, since they cost about a tenth of the price of the real thing). In spite of the company's insistence that they do not allow counterfeit goods to be sold, a United States government report named Taobao as a major offender for selling pirated merchandise.

Ma loves Taobao, as her endless purchase history clearly shows. Over the past two months, she has spent over 5,000 yuan ($787) on knock-off Ferragamo shoes, a case for her cell phone, a Japanese facial cream, a wheeled suitcase, a jacket, two dresses, and an ergonomic pillow shaped like a koala bear. She used her mother's credit card to pay for all of her purchases, since her job at the moment is an unpaid internship.

China boasts the biggest community of Internet users in the world, with over 538 million Web surfers.[2] The figure grows every month, and could potentially get much bigger since only 40% of the population currently has access to the Internet.

This group has completely changed how they access information and entertain themselves, and Internet users in China spend more hours per day online than any other country.[3] The Internet has drawn them closer to the rest of the planet, and to their fellow countrymen. Just a few years ago, residents of Harbin, in the north, had no way of following what was happening in real time in the south, except through Government-controlled media. Now they do, thanks to Weibo.

Weibo proves that some Chinese copies turn out better than the Western originals. It was conceived of as a version of Twitter, but it is much more versatile. For Ma, it's the perfect blend of Twitter and Facebook, because it allows users to share photos and video without leaving their homepage. Ma thinks that the best Chinese social media sites are more focused on a multimedia experience. When it comes to text, they have a clear advantage: a post on Weibo can have a maximum of 140 characters, but in Chinese that is long enough to tell a whole story. For Web users, the year 2011 would go down in history as the Year of Weibo, as the platform tripled its number of users, reaching 250 million.[4]

The Chinese use the Internet in proportion to their buying power. A worker from Canton is not looking for the same things as a marketing consultant in Shanghai, for example, especially since the worker probably cannot afford a computer. But if he's still single, he would probably spend one or two paychecks on the latest model cell phone. A bricklayer working at the most far-flung construction site might sleep in a rickety wooden hut with twenty other workers, but he'll have a phone that can play music and videos.[5] It's the sole source of entertainment for workers who have left behind families thousands of miles away, and work from sunup to sundown. They use their phones to listen to music, talk, play games, and look at porn sites.

Almost all Chinese Internet users have an account on QQ, the first instant-messaging service launched in the country. Its logo is a penguin with a red scarf. Migrant workers use QQ when they go to cybercafés, their favorite hang-out spot. The *wangba* (网吧), or Internet bars are great for them because they never close, they have bathrooms, heat in the winter and air conditioning in the summer. Workers go there to play computer games, alone or with other Internet users, or to take a nap. If they don't have a babysitter for their children, they may drop them off at the cybercafé, using it as daycare. The kids play computer games while their parents go to work, knowing they'll be right where they left them at the end of the day.[6]

Middle-class professionals, teachers and administrative office staff, for example, with a monthly salary of between 4,500 and 6,000 yuan ($714–$950), have their own laptop computer. They've been using QQ for years, and probably have profiles on several other social networking sites. They can go to the popular search engine Baidu to find music and books, or to dozens of similar sites. Users have free access to thousands of television shows and movies through Web sites like Tudou and Youku. Offers from restaurants and businesses selling leisure activities fill up their email inboxes, and to stay informed, they are just a click away from millions of blogs and micro-blogs. Chinese Internet users generally don't visit Western sites like Google, YouTube and Facebook, not only because of government censorship, but because of esthetic, cultural preferences. Many Chinese feel that the Western Web sites do not have their needs in mind.

Their extremely wealthy compatriots live in a world apart. They are a small minority who live surrounded by luxury and excess, and have embraced certain Western products and brands like a religion. Special Internet forums, VIP social networking sites like p1cn.com, and "members only" e-commerce sites have arisen to cater to this rarefied group. To the rich, using QQ seems low-class.

Companies compete for pieces of a pie that continues to expand.

Areas of biggest growth among Internet users are concentrated on two extremes: the upper class, and rural-urban migrants. In 2011, Tencent, the company that created QQ, launched Weixin, an application that sends instant messages for free, aiming to attract liberal, urban professionals. Users must have a QQ account before they can instant-message. Ma Chengcheng loves Weixin. The best part, she explains, is an option called "message in a bottle," where users text a message on any subject and launch it into cyberspace, hoping that a stranger responds. Ma acknowledges that everyone uses it to flirt.

Ma fits into a privileged profile: upper-middle class, urban, an avid consumer, mostly apolitical, who never goes a day without going online, and whose tastes change quickly. Her parents paid for her education, and unlike many Chinese she does not need to send money home to help support them. Basically, they still support her. At twenty-four, she has not found a job, so she takes unpaid internships for the experience.

The mutual friend who introduced us described Ma jokingly as an Internet addict. The first time just the two of us got together, Ma was leaning against a fence outside the Qianmen metro stop, in old Beijing. It was in the afternoon, around the time when many offices close, and swarms of people continuously entered and left the station. Even though she's small at barely five feet tall, her bold sense of style, a mix of modern Western and Japanese, makes her stand out in a crowd: she wore a blazer, a bright blue skirt with white moons on it, a yellow blouse, and bright red shoes that matched her handbag. "My friends say I'm the most *ku* [cool]," she said with a wink from behind her oversized, round, plastic-framed glasses.

Qianmen is Beijing's oldest neighborhood. During the Qing dynasty, visitors coming to the city to take the civil service exam would stay in the rooming houses there. It was a bohemian area, full of night owls and intellectuals, known for its theaters, operas and bordellos. Not much of the old neighborhood remains. The main street is a wide pedestrian mall, a very popular tourist destination. The storefronts have been remodeled with fake stone facades, a sacrilege to many Chinese. But Ma loves it here because there are so many Western shops. I ask where she'd like to go, and she replies without hesitation "Sim Ba Ke," the Chinese name for Starbucks. "I love the *caramel macchiato*," she says, sounding out the English pronunciation, with emphasis on the 'r' in caramel. One of her favorite activities is going to a Western café and paying 40 yuan for a coffee (over six dollars, what a cleaning person in Beijing would earn for two hours of work), listening to the same record playing over and over on the sound system.

As we order, she gets a text. "Sorry, it's my mother. She learned how to send text messages and now she's always asking me things. She wants to know where I am," Ma explains. "I talk much more with her now than I did when I lived at home." She takes a picture of herself sipping her coffee with her phone, and sends it to her mother.

Ma arrived in Beijing a year ago. Her family lives in Zhengzhou, the capital of Henan, one of the poorest rural provinces. But Zhengzhou, a city of almost nine million inhabitants, is growing quickly. With good contacts in local government, the liberal economic policies put in place in 1978 made all the difference for Ma's parents. They opened a real estate business, one of the most profitable sectors of the economy. They paid the state fine for having two daughters instead of one, as required by law. Back in the year 2000, when very few Chinese families could afford it, they bought a computer. "Some of my friends had been given one, and I asked my father if I could have one. He said yes because he thought it might be helpful with my school work."

Every night, after she did her homework, Ma would sit in front of her IBM computer screen, a dinosaur that took up half of her desk, and pursued her passion: dressing and undressing dolls. "It was a Japanese game, in a manga style. You had to choose the nicest outfit, coordinating the skirts, nylons and hats. Now it seems silly, but at the time I loved it."

I asked her if she still likes fashion, because she looks very well put together. She blushes. "It's just that I'm in the 155 Club. That's what we call ourselves on the Internet, girls who are 155 centimeters tall (five feet). We like to dress ourselves a little bit like dolls. It's kind of like the Koreans or the Japanese," she replies. She has never been to Japan or Korea, and all of her fashion and cultural references on those two countries come from the Internet. In high school, Ma discovered that the Internet was good not just for playing games, but also as a means of self-expression, and learning about the world.

At the time, Internet forums were all the rage, known in China as BBS, for the English initials for Bulletin Board Sites.[7] When Ma started high school, students went on them to exchange files and opinions. Her class, which published the school's newspaper, started a BBS to get feedback from the rest of the student body. Gradually an online community of students developed. "Everyone had their own story, and we wrote about whatever we wanted. And we told secrets, and criticized the teachers we didn't like."

The forum was a big success until their last year of high school, when the students didn't have a free minute to spare to post on it, and it was forgotten. Their only interest then was studying for the dreaded *gaokao*, the college entrance exam.

To understand why so many young Chinese get hooked on the Internet, bear in mind the enormous pressure they are under throughout secondary school. They are forewarned about the *gaokao* exam and its significance from a very young age. The competition is so fierce,[8] parents are obsessed with ensuring their children score well. They believe that if they get a high score, they will get into a top-tier university, and will land a good job after they graduate. To enhance their profiles, students participate in a range of extracurricular activities, such as calligraphy, mathematics Olympics, debate club, flute . . . the last year of high school, students generally don't get home until nine or ten o'clock at night, even on Saturdays. If they're lucky they'll have a few free hours on Sunday afternoon to go to the pool or take a walk. Romantic relationships, or spending time on anything that might detract from their studies is strictly forbidden.

The problem is that all of the sacrifices they make could result in nothing more than frustration. In 2011, almost seven million young people graduated from college, but jobs are increasingly scarce. According to some Chinese news sources, unemployment among young people hovers at around 10%, and among recent graduates, it could[9] be as high as 30%. A degree from one of the most prestigious universities can facilitate things, but they only accept the very best students from each province, and applicants from Beijing or Shanghai are always given preference.[10]

Years after graduation, most young adults still vividly remember the intense stress they experienced from the *gaokao* exam, and many still have nightmares about it. Ma tells me the year she spent preparing for the exam was utterly miserable. She practiced hard at the piano, even though she hated it. Every day, she attended a *buxiban*, a test prep course, for mathematics and English, but all she got from the constant studying was eye strain and a prescription for glasses, she didn't score high enough on the test to get into the University of Beijing. She swore she would never study so hard for anything else ever again.

Her head hanging low and feeling incredibly guilty, she went to

Zhengzhou University. She would have liked to studied fashion design, but she didn't want to let her parents down any more than she already had, so she entered their Economics and International Business school. The only thing she asked her parents was that they let her live on-campus. She happily gave up her own room at home so she could share a hundred square feet with three other girls: Qian Jing, from Jiangsu; Feng Li Lei, from Shandong; and Xin Xiang, from Henan.

They were inseparable. They came from very different places, but they shared a common aversion for rote memorization and following rules. Qian Jing was the only one who had already experienced living away from home, since she had gone to a boarding school, the other three were ecstatic to finally be on their own. Studying wasn't their top priority. For the first year, it's not unusual for new students to largely avoid the classrooms.

The four fast friends barricaded themselves in their new living quarters, which included two bunk beds, four small desks, and four computers which were always on, twenty-four hours a day. They did everything together. The girls got up at six in the morning, and went out to the yard to participate in the obligatory calisthenics exercises, following the routine called out over the loudspeakers. Then they took showers in the group bathroom, and retreated to their room until the next morning. They didn't even go down to the dining room. They bought fruit, skewers of chicken and sesame seed rolls at a small store on campus. They kept their computers connected to the Internet all night to download television shows and watch them the next day. Without even getting out of bed, they discovered what people their age were like in the United States, South Korea and Japan; they vicariously experienced passionate love stories, and cried over far-away tragedies. "We didn't leave our room. We didn't really like the other students, and the campus was on the outskirts of the city, so there wasn't anything to do around there. We had just gotten out of high school, where the teachers control you all the time. For the first time, I was experiencing freedom."

The education system is the subject of recurring debate in the Chinese media. "Students are overworked." "They only learn how to memorize, not how to be creative." "They focus so much on studying they don't see anything else, they're immature, unable to relate to people and solve problems." Professors and psychologists make these points loudly and often. In their opinion, parents are so obsessed with their children's academic preparation, they fail to provide sufficient emotional support. Ma says her parents neglected to provide any kind of education on romantic and sexual relationships. Luckily for her, she had the Internet.

She learned the basics from the *wangluo xiaoshuo*, stories that writers uploaded onto the Internet themselves, a phenomenon that was very popular in the first decade of 2000. It was the only way for many young writers to get their work read, and to get past the censors. Everyone wrote under a pseudonym, but some had millions of readers. They uploaded works of historical fiction, science fiction, romantic comedy, and erotica, an extremely popular category, which the Government never would have allowed to go into print. Ma was especially interested in the homosexual love stories. "I'm not attracted to women, but I was very curious about romantic relationships between people of the same gender. Those were the stories I read the most, really, because I knew I'd never be able to buy them in any bookstore," she admits with a laugh. As she talks, she has a tic: she takes a lock of hair between her fingers and tugs on it, just a little, as if just for an instant she wanted to make sure she wasn't wearing a wig.

In that first year of college, she made many virtual friends who she never met in person. She only talked to them on the Internet. The social networking sites that were modeled after Facebook, like Kaixin and Ren Ren, were the most *huo* (popular) among the students. "My roommates and I would send messages for hours, not talking, each one with her own laptop. We even liked to send messages to each other that way," she recalls. "Chat allows for more privacy than a forum. It's easier to talk, because you can just be yourself, and you don't get embarrassed. You feel different writing, and since it's immediate, it's much more fun. Instead of talking face to face, we did it back to back," she laughs.

"Use the Internet in a civilized way. Stay out of the cyber-cafés. Stopping Internet addiction begins with yourself."

This public service announcement can be found in many Chinese schools, written in white characters over a red background. The unprecedented freedom the Web offers presents a continuous challenge to the government. Each year in China, more than a hundred thousand demonstrations take place,[11] protesting everything from corruption to toxic waste. Before the proliferation of blogs, authorities could generally control the protests, because they were isolated incidents. But, what happens when protests can be organized in an online forum, or promoted on Weibo?

Beijing is not standing by with crossed arms. In 1996, a year after the commercial use of the Internet was permitted, the government began to censure it. Over sixty laws were enacted allowing the state to oversee and censure content. In 2003, the government solidified its control in a project popularly known as the Second Great Wall of China, or the Great Firewall. It's like an octopus with many tentacles. First, it defines a list of terms prohibited from local search engines such as Baidu or Sohu. The list of censured words and terms is long, and includes: "dictatorship," "work reeducation," "Tibetan independence," "Xinjiang independence," "Falun Gong," and the names of the most well-known dissidents. An email that contains one of those terms rarely reaches its destination. The Great Firewall manipulates the results of certain searches: if a user wants to find information on Tiananmen, they will only see photos of tourists in the plaza, never images from the 1989 Tiananmen massacre.[12]

And they can't access Web sites on foreign servers that the government doesn't want them to see. Web sites of dissidents in exile such as Boxun, human rights organization's Web sites including Human Rights China, and some English-language news sites are unavailable. Lastly, the government requires foreign corporations that have Web sites in China to modify their content[13] and to provide them with information on Web users searching the Internet for censured information.[14]

In addition to these and other systems in place, there is a large cadre of Internet police monitoring the Web. Some sources estimate there are thirty thousand of them, but no official data exists to corroborate this. To foreigners living in China, especially journalists, this monolithic censorship apparatus makes it much more difficult to do their jobs. To the Chinese, it can destroy their lives: several bloggers have been sentenced to between one and two years of prison, just for comments they posted on the Internet.[15]

Beijing does more than simply block certain Web sites. Its propaganda machine churns out content. Thousands of volunteers receive five mao, half a yuan (seven cents) for every comment favorable to the government that they post on social media. They have been disparagingly dubbed the 50-Cent Party (*wumaodang*). Many schools and local Communist Party youth groups have people dedicated to posting messages on Web sites, echoing the official party message, and denouncing other posters who get out of line. They use false profiles on social media, to drown out activists, or to make friends with them in order to get information.

Official Chinese media outlets must operate within narrowly drawn parameters. With very few exceptions, they simply serve as mouthpieces for the government. In the first decade of 2000, they were directed to publish stories informing the public on the dangers of the Internet. Several deadly fires in cybercafés illustrated the lack of security in those establishments, where young people supposedly would end up wasting their lives away, mindlessly playing games and looking at pornography. In 2006, the Party Youth described Internet cafes as "nests of juvenile crime and depravation." Tens of thousands of *wangba* were shut down, to allegedly avoid "a serious social problem that could threaten the nation's future."

The notion that the Internet could corrupt young people was gaining traction among the general public. Several true stories added flame to the fire: a teenager killed his parents because they wouldn't let him spend more time on the Internet, and several young people died in provinces across the country after spending days at a time glued to their computer screens, playing games continuously without taking a break. Panic spread. China became the first country in the world to define Internet addiction as a disease, and rehabilitation facilities sprung up where young people were subjected to the strictest discipline measures.[16] For eight thousand yuan per month (around $1,300), these centers guarantee success rates of between seventy and eighty percent.

It is estimated that there are between three and four hundred Internet addiction treatment centers in China. They refer to themselves as camps, but some seem more like prisons. They have bars on the windows, and are located within military complexes. The residents must wear uniforms, are forbidden from using telephones or computers during their stay, and must adhere to the dictated schedules. This does not raise any eyebrows in China, where all university students are required to attend a military camp for several weeks out of the year. They get up at five o'clock in the morning, exercise strenuously throughout the day, with little to eat, and can only take showers a few times. This is part of what the Chinese call *chi ku* (吃苦), "eating bitterness," which teaches one to withstand life's hardships and unpleasantries. "Suffering can help you to get better," one of the camps asserts in its promotional materials.

Suspicions began to arise when it became known that these camps medicated those held there, and in some cases even administered electroshock treatments. The psychiatrist Yang Yongxin, known as "Uncle Yang," and director of an Internet addiction treatment program in a Shandong hospital, created this treatment method. According to various news sources, he subjected almost three thousand teenagers to electroshock therapy to cure them of their supposed addiction. He called it *xing nao*, "waking up the brain." Eventually it was discovered that Yang did not actually hold a degree in psychotherapy. The pressure from the media was so great that in July 2010 the Ministry of Health issued a statement confirming that the use of electroshock therapy in treating Internet addiction was strictly prohibited, since it had not been demonstrated to have any known therapeutic effects.

The loudest alarm was set off by the case of Deng Senshan, a fifteen-year-old boy who died just one day after his parents sent him to an Internet addiction treatment camp in the province of Guangxi. According to witnesses, an instructor forced Deng to run laps in the yard to the point of utter exhaustion. When he collapsed on the ground, the instructor brutally beat him. He was admitted to the hospital with contusions and internal bleeding, and died within a few hours. Thirteen people were arrested. Later, it was revealed that the center had operated without a license, and without qualified staff.

The fallout was significant. Other cases of abuse at the camps came to light. Once again, the authorities acknowledged that there was no system in place to register and control these kinds of treatment camps. Many bloggers pointed out that teenagers were being labeled as "addicts" in order to scare the general public away from the Web.

I n China, anyone who spends at least six hours a day on the Internet for three months and cannot relate to people normally qualifies as an addict. According to this definition, Ma Chencheng has been addicted since she started college. "That's ridiculous! I'm shy, but I'm normal. You can't generalize like that. A lot of people use the Internet to escape from the world because it gives them security, and free entertainment. . . . It's true that some people really are addicted and need treatment, but the majority are just normal people. On the other hand, there are a lot of disturbed people who don't go on the Internet. Who should be locked up?"

The way Ma sees it, the authorities demonize the Internet because it allows people to express themselves like never before, and because it offers an alternative information source beyond the official state-sponsored media. Citizens are no longer handcuffed to the government on the Web.

Between 2009 and 2010, the government shutdown 1.3 million sites as part of an official campaign to combat "pornography and vulgarity."[17] The definition of what is "pornographic" (*huang*, 黃) is ambiguous. It has to do with what is immoral, but also what is ideologically unacceptable. In the same purge, pages with violent content, homosexual forums, blogs on democracy, and sites with artwork featuring nudes were all deleted.

But a double-standard exists. Newsstands don't sell porn, but they do sell magazines like *Nanren Zhuang* ("For Him"), with a monthly circulation of 480,000, published by none other than the National Tourism Board, featuring on the cover photos of actresses in lingerie, soaking wet like they just stepped out of the shower. Passionate kisses in movies do not make it past the censors, but sex shops keep springing up in virtually every neighborhood. "We need a clear definition of "pornography" in order to justify a campaign against it. The laws and regulations only make vague references. The authorities censure what they themselves consider pornographic," Zhang Cong, a magazine editor in Beijing complained on the official Web site China.org.[18]

Some content from the BBC and CNN is considered pornographic to government authorities in Beijing. When these networks talk about dissidents, demonstrations, or any other subject that makes them uncomfortable, they cut off the signal. Suddenly the television screen goes black, and the picture doesn't return for several minutes, until the censors feel the danger has passed and it is safe to resume the broadcast.

Internet users constantly create new ways to empower themselves. They call it *fang qiang*, "breaking down the wall." They are real magicians when it comes to word play, and in a kind of collective catharsis, they subversively mock the absurdities of the system.[19] There are hundreds of examples of rebellion on the Internet. Two of the most widely known feature animals: the grass-mud horse, and the fresh-water or river crab. Although they are written with different characters, "grass-mud horse" is pronounced *"cao ni ma,"* and sounds very similar to one of the worst insults that exists in Chinese, directed at someone's mother. The river crab is also very popular, because it is pronounced *"he xie,"* which sounds very similar to the Chinese word for "harmonize," the government's euphemistic term for censorship. Web surfers use these imaginative terms to make fun of the regime, and to get around the security filters. For example, to find information on the Web about censorship, or to find out what Web sites have been "harmonized," type "river crab" into a Chinese search engine.

The crab and the grass-mud horse can be found all over the Web, in pictures, T-shirts, songs, and even stuffed animals. But the anticensorship menagerie includes many more creatures: there are "intestinal worms," "Franco-Croatian squid," "lucky traveling cats," "whales with outstretched tails," "singing geese," and "smart, fragrant chickens". The names for these one-of-a-kind animals sound very similar to the words for "anal sex," the English phrase "fuck you," "pubic hair," "tampon," "vaginal infection," and "masturbation." Chinese Internet users love to taunt and provoke. Even apolitical Web surfers like Ma appreciate these kinds of jokes. She doesn't use the Internet as a means to criticize the government; she attributes the aspects of her country that she doesn't like to a state of underdevelopment. What does bother her a great deal is the paternalistic nature of the censorship, which keeps her from visiting all the sites she wants to. She loves Fanfou, a Twitter copycat that had over a million users when the government abruptly shut it down in the summer of 2009, because it had posted information about the uprising in Xinjiang.[20] This attempt on the state's part to preserve a moral purity which doesn't exist strikes Ma as pathetic.

"People are always going to find a way to see the Web sites they want to see," she asserts. Many of her friends have a VPN, or virtual private network, which they access through the Internet. It functions as a kind of tunnel, that safeguards privacy. "But the government isn't worried about young people in the cities, they understand we know how to get around censorship and we just buy pirated DVDs when they ban a movie. They are worried about unfiltered information getting out to the masses of poor people."

She wanted to meet for lunch at one of her favorite spots in Beijing, a huge shopping mall called The Village. It's located in Sanlitun, a neighborhood frequented by expatriates and upper-class Chinese ever since the foreign embassies were first relocated there in 1950. In the midnineties, the city's first bar opened in the area. Today it's the focal point of Beijing night-life, although outdoor cafes and indie-rock concerts have given way to discos and chain restaurants and stores. For many, it has lost its unique flavor.

Several sleek, postmodern buildings comprise the shopping district. There are restaurants, cineplexes, and flagship stores of the most widely recognized international brands. Ma and her friends like to go there and window-shop whenever they have some free time. They buy coffees and walk around. If they have some money to spend, they'll go to the Queen's Café, a famous restaurant chain that began in Hong Kong. The first one opened its doors on the island in 1952. The chain serves up a peculiar culinary mix, because the owner, Yu Yong Fu, learned to cook under a Russian chef.

The restaurant is packed, and Edith Piaf's voice wafts through the sound system. We count seven tables with people staring down at their iPads. Young urban Chinese with some money to spend like to take their entire families out to dinner there. The decor is a blend of classic Chinese style and what some locals understand to be Western style. Empty wine bottles with plastic roses in them adorn the tables, lacy curtains drape over the windows. We sat under a medieval-looking lamp. Ma takes a folding hair brush from her bag and carefully brushes her bangs. "With this wind, my hair's always a mess," she explains. She orders a combination plate with chicken, and spaghetti with tomato sauce, with bubble tea to drink, very typical of the south.

Ma's happy because she has the day off, and she has been putting in very long hours lately. The investment firm where she interns never closes. And people even go in to the office on the weekend, to tie up loose ends. "The pace is horrible, but people fight to get a job there." Ma got her internship through her uncle, who works for an investment bank. When she graduated from the university, with her degree in hand and some knowledge of English, she thought she'd be deluged with job offers. But Ma found out there were hundreds of thousands of recent college grads with better resumes and more experience. Her uncle advised her to work for no pay for a few months. To save money on rent, she lives with him and his wife. "We're not very close, but we get along alright," she says. "His apartment is big, and I have my own room. Most of the time I hang out in my room with my laptop."

We had left off talking about the slang that had developed on the Internet. Ma opens Tianya.com on her computer. "See how they're talking about the *yueguangzu* here? It's a popular term right now. It means people who spend everything they earn every month, without saving anything. That's what happens to me," she says with a laugh. In recent years, names for everything have sprung up, putting a label on dozens of urban tribes: there are the ants (*yizu*), college graduates who live in rooms in the basements of buildings in the major cities because they can't afford to rent a room above ground; the mortgage slaves (*fang nu*); the slaves to their own children (*hai nu*); couples that get married and divorced from one day to the next (*shan hun zu*); and many others which essentially reflect the main sources of middle-class angst: the struggle to earn enough money to buy a car, an apartment, and start a family.

More than just isolated terms have begun circulating on the Internet, a whole language has taken root. It's the *huo xing wen*, or "Martian language," that started in Taiwan in 2005. It could not be any more cryptic: in order to write it, one must substitute the Chinese characters for their homophones, or for symbols, numbers, sounds in English, or Japanese ideograms. For example, the number 0 is the equivalent of the preposition "without." It's exquisitely complex, and its creators want to keep it that way, because it is meant to be used to communicate in code. It has grown so popular that now there are even "Martian-Chinese" dictionaries. Ma does not know how to write in Martian, but her younger sister does. "Every time I go home, she shows me new Web sites and forums. The people who were born in the nineties are the ones changing the Internet, not us," she explains. "They are really bored, and they keep inventing new things all the time. But don't underestimate the Internet generation. We have a lot of power."

They do indeed. They can exert some influence over the courts, as they did in the 2009 scandal involving Deng Yujiao, a twenty-one-year-old woman who worked as a pedicurist in a hotel in Badong, in the middle of the country. A local official tried to rape her, and she fought him off with a knife, fatally stabbing him. She initially received the death sentence for homicide, but luckily for her the case became known and was talked about all over the Internet. Outraged, millions of people posted messages of support. T-shirts with her name on them were handed out for free, and she became a national heroine, a victim of the abuse of power. Finally, the court upheld the guilty verdict, but exempted her from the death penalty because of "mental disturbance." Five years ago, a case that no one outside of the province would have ever heard of became a national headline, thanks to the Internet.

For years, Internet users have practiced a particular method of collective justice. It's known as *renrou sousuo* (人肉搜索) which literally translates as the "human flesh search engine." It is called this because people themselves manually perform the searches, not computer programs. They dig up information on people who have committed a crime or who have behaved offensively, unearthing every last detail about them, and then post it on the Internet to alert the whole world. That is what happened with a powerful member of the local government in Shenzhen, who tried to sexually abuse a girl in a restaurant. The security cameras captured the moment when the young girl ran out of the men's bathroom, where the government official had taken her. Next the video shows the girl's father looking for his daughter's attacker, and the official confronting him and offering him money to keep him quiet. Someone posted the video on the Web site Netease. The *renrou sousuo* had only just begun. "Can you see how proud of himself he seems?" One comment read. "He's a dead man." "Another official abusing the public," exclaimed another. The official was subsequently fired.

The *renrou sousuo* made life impossible for Wang Jiao, a nurse from Hangzhou. In 2006, something inspired her to post a video of herself on the Internet showing her bludgeoning a kitten to death with the heel of her shoe. Thousands of disgusted people started interfering in her life. They posted her address, pictures of her, and where she worked on the Web. She eventually turned herself in to the police. Along with the person who had shot the video, she lost her job and had to move away to another city.

Some experts warn that the *renrou sousuo* could unleash witch hunts, and destroy the lives of people who have not committed any crime, no matter how offensive their behavior may seem. They believe that as long as citizens can exercise this kind of vigilante justice while no meaningful institutional changes are made, it will not lead to a more just society.[21] So far, only corrupt government officials at the provincial level have been singled out for criticism; officials on the national level have gone unscathed.

After lunch, we go out for a walk. The wind has died down, so Ma isn't worried about her hair. We see the latest graphic novel by Zhu Deyong in a bookstore window, and Ma runs in to buy it. The Taiwanese author had immediate success with his series loosely based on the American television show "Sex in the City," called *Fen Hong Se Nu Lang* (Pink Ladies), cataloging the hilarious exploits of four roommates in Taipei. It was such a hit, his graphic novels were adapted for television. In contrast to the American series, the Chinese protagonists are devoid of cheesy cuteness; they are neurotic, caustic and selfish.

The comic Ma buys is titled "Everyone is Sick." As the author explains in the introduction, he aims to illustrate through humor the ills of contemporary society. In his view, the problem many Asians have is that, after collectively experiencing widespread poverty, now wealth is destroying them. "I love the way he sees life," Ma says, flipping through the pages. "We all have our neuroses, our quirks. At least on the Internet you can find other people like you," she jokes.

We sit down on a bench to people-watch. In the middle of the Sanlitun shopping district, there is an area with rows of fountains jetting up from the pavement in a grid. Some children wait expectantly for them to go on. When they do, they run around chasing each other among the streams of water, squealing with delight. A few feet away, a model wearing an electric-blue Lycra outfit strikes a pose for two fashion photographers.

I ask Ma what direction she thinks the Internet is heading in her country. There are rumors that the government is going to require Weibo users to provide their personal information, and in the past few months they have experienced a decline in users.[22] "I have no idea," Ma answers. "But if it's not Weibo, it will be some other Web site. Everything's moving so fast.... The Internet here follows its own path, that's why sometimes the Western companies aren't successful. For example, if Facebook came to China, it wouldn't do well. People already use the copycat version, Ren Ren, and that's not even very popular. My sister has never gone on Facebook. We'll see what happens with the censorship. Maybe it will disappear, or maybe it will get even more restrictive. I'm optimistic."

I want to know what she thinks of Chinese Web surfers who are in jail or under house arrest, like Cheng Jianping, a woman who disappeared in October 2010, on her wedding day. Ten days earlier, she had retweeted a message on Twitter in which the original author, Cheng's fiancé Hua Chunhui, satirically suggested that Chinese people should attack the Japanese Pavilion in the Shanghai Expo. At the time, tensions between China and Japan were running high over the Diayou Islands, which the Japanese call the Senkaku Islands, and both countries claim as their own. According to Amnesty International, Cheng was sentenced to one year of "reeducation through labor" for "disturbing the social order."

"I read something about that, but honestly I don't get into those issues," Ma says. "This is a very big country, with very many people. Censorship has historical, political causes," she explains thoughtfully. Like many young upper-class Chinese, she believes a certain level of control is necessary to ensure that the uneducated masses don't "get into trouble" and to keep rumors from going around the Web.

"You know," she says, "even though China is one of the countries that controls people the most, the United States does it too, in a more sophisticated way, and its companies store much more information on its citizens than anyone else in the world.[23] I just think that the cultural level of the poor peasants here makes it impossible for them to assimilate certain things." I ask if she thinks only rich people should have free access to the Internet. "Many just things are built on injustices," she sighs, as she takes two heart-shaped lollipops from her bag and offers me one.

8

〈〈〈〈〈〈

A Prostitute in Secret

Mrs. Zhen enjoys choral singing more than anything. She loves how her husky voice blends in with all the others. So every morning she goes to the Temple of Heaven, and sings with an amateur chorus. She brings along a thermos of tea, and a visor to wear in case the sun is strong, and walks to the park of the same name in the southern part of the city. Some of her fellow singers who gather in the park take it very seriously, bringing along amplifiers and microphones, practicing every day, and attracting hundreds of curious onlookers. But Zhen doesn't want to call attention to herself. She prefers singing with smaller groups, with just six or seven people. They stand under the shade of some trees, and follow along with sheet music, so no one gets lost. When it's time to sing *The East is Red*,[1] Zhen sings her heart out. It's the high point of her day.

In the early morning hours, the park is bustling. People gather to do calisthenics, play musical instruments, play chess, fly kites. . . . Many Chinese retire when they're only sixty years old.[2]

The average life expectancy is seventy-five, leaving several years for most retirees to enjoy. Although the pensions are low, this generation of seniors for the most part were born into poverty, and are used to enjoying no-cost recreation and pastimes outside in the fresh air.

Zhen returns home at midday. She buys fresh vegetables and eggs from a street cart. When she's not working, she takes a nap on the sofa after lunch. If a client calls, she takes a shower and does her make-up, getting ready for work. At forty-four, she's more tired than she used to be, and she's decided to only sleep with one man a day.

P rostitution is illegal in China, but it can easily be found in bath houses, hotels, karaoke bars, hair salons and massage parlors. According to the United Nations, there are at least four million women working as prostitutes in China. There are also men who prostitute themselves (known as "ducks") and gigolos who entertain wealthy women in discos, but their numbers are much smaller.

When the Communists won the civil war in 1949, they ordered local governments to eradicate prostitution. To them, it was a form of oppression because poor women had no other alternative than to sell their bodies in order to survive, and that had no place in the New China. In cities like Shanghai, where the sex industry had taken off after the second Sino-Japanese War (1937–1945), the authorities put many programs in place to socially integrate prostitutes. By the early sixties, the government claimed they had successfully shot down the oldest profession in the world. Actually it had just gone underground. After the economic liberalization of 1978, the sex industry emerged from hiding, and grew, becoming one of the most lucrative sectors of the economy.

Like Chinese society itself, prostitution in China conforms to a pyramid structure. At the top are the *baoernai*, (包二奶), women kept by wealthy businessmen and high-level government officials. They are a status symbol, similar to the concubines of the imperial age, and their lovers whisk them away for weekends at island resorts, take them out to expensive restaurants, buy them cars (some sporty compact models are known as "second wives' cars") and buy them apartments, where the men visit them once in a while. In Shenzhen, in the southeast, entire residential developments are filled with women kept by Hong Kong businessmen. The *baoernai* have such tremendous buying power, they are specifically marketed to by the luxury brands.

One step down on the pyramid are the girls who work in nightclubs catering to the rich and the *baopo* (包婆), who accompany their clients on trips, and escort them to parties or special events. Many of these women have master's degrees and speak foreign languages, and want to make contacts among the powerful in business and government while earning some extra money. They understand that once they're over thirty, they won't be in such high demand. If they stay in the world of prostitution, they tend to slide down a level on the scale, joining the ranks of the *santing* (三厅), women who work in karaoke bars, restaurants and tea houses. They have to drink, dance and talk with the men, and sleep with them if the men pay for it.

There are also prostitutes working in most hotels. They are known as *dingdong xiaojie* (叮咚小姐), or "ding-dong girls", since they ring the doorbells of the rooms and offer their services. They work for the hotels or reach an agreement with them. When a man checks into one of these establishments, he knows that most likely within five minutes of unpacking his suitcase, a young woman will be at the door of his room, offering to give him a "special massage."

A step further down are the *falangmei*, (发廊妹) or prostitutes who work in beauty salons. There are two types of hair salons in

China: ones that actually offer haircuts, and the ones that special-ize in other services. They are easy to tell apart, because while the sex shops have red, white, and blue neon signs in their windows just like the real salons, the workers inside are practically naked. Those women charge very little, barely a hundred yuan (fifteen dollars) per service, and they need to have more customers each day to make it to the end of the month. Many do not use condoms, because their clients refuse, and their bosses pressure them not to.

Streetwalkers are at the bottom of the pyramid. The *jienü* (街女) are the least attractive, or the oldest who can no longer get work in a nightclub. They solicit customers in parks or near con-struction sites. The women who have pimps have to obey them, but they suffer fewer attacks and violence from customers.

The poorest streetwalkers only charge five dollars for their ser-vices. If they're really desperate, they may barter for food, or a night's lodging. They work wherever they can: in the street, under bridges, among the trees. They cannot afford contraceptives or doctor's visits, and depend completely on the NGOs for health services. They are the first to fall victim to sexually transmitted diseases and violence, often at the hands of the police.

Because of her age, Zhen would most likely fall into this cate-gory of women working the streets. With any luck, she might as-pire to be a Madam at a club. But two years ago, she had a stroke of good fortune. A long-time client who works in real estate and owns several properties in Beijing became her protector. The ar-rangement is straightforward: Zhen lives in one of his apartments rent-free, and she can continue to see other clients. She just has to give him preference whenever he calls her.

I met Zhen through Wu Rong Rong, a sociologist and expert in gender equality and prostitution. When I told her Wu had sug-gested I give her a call, Zhen invited me to come to her home, in a middle-class neighborhood in the south of the city. When she opened her door, a succulent aroma wafted out into the hallway. "I was cooking," she said with a smile. "You're just in time to eat."

The living room was spotless, equipped with all the necessities: a DVD player, radio, television, and fan. A collection of stuffed animals, including a five-foot-high Bambi, filled a large blue armchair. Zhen gestured for me to sit down, and brought two glasses of hot water. "It will be ready in a minute," she said, and hurried back into the kitchen to stir the pot.

Zhen is of medium height, with a small waist and large breasts. She has a broad face, with rosy cheeks, and a constant smile, which accentuates the smile lines around her eyes. She has not yet turned forty-five, but she looks older. She still knows how to play the coquette: she wears her hair curled, and dyed brown. That day she wore a black lace dress with a pink lining underneath, and sandals with two-inch heels.

"So Wu told you about me, right? Wu is a good friend. I haven't seen her in a while, but she's been a big help to me," she explained, setting down a dish overflowing with beans and steaming tofu on the table. "First, let's eat," she said maternally, "then we can talk." When we had finished, she brought a dish of grapes out, took her shoes off, and settled into an easy chair. I asked if I could turn on the digital recorder, and she nodded.

She summed up her life story. She had grown up in a town in Chongqing, in central China.[3] Her parents worked the land, and it fell to her to look after her four younger siblings. Every morning, they walked along a roadside for two hours to get to school. Their family could not afford shoes, so they walked barefoot. When she was thirteen, she carried her baby brother along on her back. She could only attend three or four hours of school each day, because after that her brother would urinate, or start to cry from hunger. When she turned fourteen, she had to drop out of school so she could help her parents. At twenty-three, she married a neighbor boy, and gave birth to a son right away. They raised pigs and farmed, but they did not earn enough money to make a living, so in 1993 she decided to try her luck in Beijing.

"Are you still married?" I asked.

"Yes, of course. But my husband doesn't know what I do," she replied, chewing a grape. "He thinks I've worked at different jobs, in a shop, selling train tickets, in restaurants. . . . He doesn't ask what I do, either. He's never been to Beijing."

"Do you think about him?"

"No," she sighs. "We have been apart for many years, and we're not a couple anymore. We call each other every once in a while, when we have to tell each other something, but he doesn't ask anything of me, and I don't ask anything of him. He tends the land and sells the vegetables at the market. He has a pick-up truck. I paid for our son's education, he just graduated with a degree in Logistical Engineering. In Chongqing, the migrants who support their families are us women. Have you ever been there? In Sichuan, the province next to ours, it's the same thing: the men play *mahjong* and drink tea, while the women cook and do the laundry," she says with a laugh.

She loves to talk. As we ate the grapes, she told me she had not gotten divorced because once she had seen something on television about how it can traumatize children. Her overriding concern, she insists, was to provide her son with the education and things she never had as a child, so she had to make money. And go to Beijing.

She wasn't frightened by the idea of moving thousands of miles away from home. She was single-mindedly focused on making as much money as she could. When she arrived in the capital, she juggled different jobs: working as an assistant in a clinic, waiting tables in a restaurant, selling false receipts (people buy them to avoid paying taxes). . . . She survived, but the work was sporadic, and didn't allow her to let her guard down, much less live comfortably. Until finally in the late nineties, foreign X-rated movies arrived in China. She made much more money selling them on video than she had selling false receipts, and men eagerly grabbed them out of her hands. But it carried much more risk. After a few months, she was arrested. "I had really bad luck. If I had only had two or three movies on me, they wouldn't have done anything, but they caught me with seven. I spent a year and a half in jail."

The Xizhimen prison, in the western area of Beijing, was a dirty, mold-infested one-story building. She was locked in a cell with twenty other women. Some of her cellmates were prostitutes, others had been convicted of trafficking contraband. They ate their meals and took care of their personal needs in the same room. The room was dark, and very cold. Her family spent 20,000 yuan ($3,100 USD), all the savings they had, in bribes to get her out of prison.

Once she was released, she didn't dare go back to selling pornographic movies. A woman she had met in prison proposed that she start working with her as a prostitute. Working in a restaurant, she could earn sixty-five dollars a month. She could earn thirty-three dollars at least sleeping with just one man. "It seemed like a good idea. And when I found out how much I could make, I didn't want to do anything else. Keep in mind that a woman could make a lot of money as a prostitute ten years ago. There weren't so many of us, and we could pick and choose our clients." She was already over thirty, but she could charge 500 yuan per session, about eighty-six dollars. She earned 6,000 yuan a month: $953, more than many engineers made. "Today that would be impossible. But some prostitutes played dirty. They swindled men, or stole their wallets. This hurt all of us, because there were more complaints, and the police started to be very hard on us."

To Zhen, Beijing was a jungle in the nineties, traumatized by the Tiananmen Square massacre, inflation and rampant unemployment. "The police were watching everybody, to make sure no one got out of line. Getting detained was very common." The movies of the sixth generation of Chinese filmmakers[4] reflect the environment Zhen inhabited, with the added pressure of having to send money home to her family.

"They would often drag us down to the police station. And the police played tricks on us. Once, another girl from my town and I were taken into custody, even though we hadn't done anything. When they presented us to the police chief, he said we were too ugly and to take us back, that he had asked for pretty girls, you can imagine for what. And there was one officer, now retired, who slept with a lot of us and never paid us. He had our phone numbers and would call us up once in a while. A real horrible person."

At the time, Zhen was living in a hovel made of brick with a corrugated metal roof in an alley in central Beijing. She received her clients there, and washed up afterward in the communal bathrooms. In the winters, temperatures could plunge to four degrees Fahrenheit, so she had to sleep with her coat on. She drank gallons of hot water with medicinal herbs to stave off urinary tract infections.

She had good relationships with some of her clients, who would give her gifts of fruit, tea or some extra money for her son. That's how she got involved with the construction contractor who, after seven years of sporadic encounters, offered to let her live in one of the apartments he owned. And that's how Mrs. Zhen came to have heat, running water, and floral curtains hanging in the windows.

She thinks of him as a friend, not a client. He's fifty years old, and married with a twenty-four-year-old daughter. He works near Huangshan, the Yellow Mountain, in Anhui, and only occasionally comes to the capital. Their arrangement is imminently practical: he doesn't mind that Zhen keeps working as a prostitute, but when he comes to Beijing, it is understood that they will meet in the apartment. "My friend has a very hard time communicating with his wife. They have lived apart for quite a while, because he works in another province," Zhen explained. "At first he would call me up to talk, and he'd spend time with me to have some company. Over the years, we grew closer, and he started to take me out to dinner. He's not rich, but he pays attention to details. He gave me a ring for my birthday. When I want to go home for the New Year, he always offers to buy my train ticket. He doesn't pay me like a regular client. If his business is doing well, he gives me some money. If I'm coming up short one month, he'll give me 500 yuan. When we sleep together, we don't talk about money. It's not the most important part of our relationship."

"How would you describe your relationship?" I asked.

"I like him very much. He's a great man, very honest. He has always helped me when I needed it, but we're not going to divorce our spouses. We both have children and respect each other's families. For example, I never call him, in case he's with his wife. Sometimes she calls him when we're together, and he has to head home in a hurry. I understand. But whenever we argue, I tell him I'm not his wife and he's not my husband, we don't belong to each other. I don't know how long it's going to last, because everything comes to an end sooner or later. But I do know that as long as I'm in Beijing, he'll always help me out."

They share the same difficult experience of being absentee parents, even though they've worked themselves to the bone for their kids. He barely talks to his daughter. Most of all, Mrs. Zhen is proud of having paid for her son's university tuition, but she would cut off her right arm before telling him how she earned the money. "If he ever found out what I did for a living, he would turn his back on me. It would be a disaster," she said, very serious.

"Now he's used to living without me. I left when he was just four years old, and his grandmother raised him, spoiling him rotten. When she died, my husband took charge, and he spoiled him too. He never learned how to do any housework. He's very immature. Whenever I go back to our village, I wear very simple, modest clothes, so he doesn't suspect what I do, and so he'll be proud of me. But he always treats me like I owe him something. He seems like one of those modern men who drinks wine and knows how to talk, but they never really listen. His friends say he's smart, and a good person. But I haven't been able to have a good relationship with him," she lamented.

Even though they weren't close, Zhen kept on saving after her son graduated, this time to buy him an apartment. She knew that as a homeowner, he'd have a much easier time finding a wife. She saved up 430,000 yuan ($68,000) for a new apartment in Chongqing, which he has never appreciated. "Once we had a fight, and he spat out everything he'd been keeping inside," Zhen remembers sadly. "Did you ever go to one single parents' conference at school? He shouted. What were my teacher's names? Did you ever do my laundry? What have you ever given me in life? I told him I had worked for him and him alone, that I had bought him the apartment so that he could try to find a wife without any worries. He answered that it wasn't necessary."

Not jail, not all the abuse she has endured, not all the years living in the hovel have beaten Zhen down. The one thing that is truly devastating to her is that her son never calls her on the phone.

According to her calculations, Zhen has only spent about 2% of her lifetime earnings on herself. Once she finished paying off her son's tuition and his apartment, she discovered she was now too old to command high rates, and could only charge 100 yuan per session. "The competition is brutal. At most, we long-timers can only hope to sleep with blue-collar workers," she says. "The rich guys want twenty-year-olds with firm butts, even though they're inexperienced and don't know how to put themselves together. The new girls are charging very little, between fifty and sixty yuan (seven to nine dollars) at Dongdan Park. We can't compete. The other day I was with some sisters who hadn't worked at all for three days.[5] They told me a lot of peasant women from the country are coming to Beijing to try to make a living. When they don't find any work, they become prostitutes. How are we going to survive?"

Since she can't compete with the younger women, for a while she has acted as an intermediary, or Madam, between them and the men she knows. She earns between twenty and thirty percent commission. And she still entertains her long-time clients, treating them very well so they'll keep coming back. Sometimes a few days can pass when no one calls her, and then she gets worried. Her friend insists on helping her out so she can make it to the end of the month. But Zhen wants to depend on him as little as possible, so she tries not to spend money. When her girlfriends in the profession tell her they're going to get together at a restaurant, she hesitates. Sometimes she'll go meet them afterward to dance or play cards. And she doesn't go shopping. Her clients give her new clothes as New Year's gifts, so that's her wardrobe. The one thing she would not dream of giving up is going to sing in the mornings. The best investment she ever made, she says, has been the 100 yuan (fifteen dollars) annual fee that lets her sing in all of the parks in Beijing.

Zhen has always worked for herself, to avoid the pimps' "shady business." But she understands that what are known as sex towns, where the mafias operate, comprise a significant portion of her industry. There are dozens of them throughout Beijing, but it's important to know how to navigate them to stay out of danger, or even just so people will talk to her. I ask her to take me along to one, but she doesn't want to be seen around there. She suggests that I talk to our friend in common, Wu Rong Rong. She knows how and when to gain entry into one of these zones. I called her that night. "Are you crazy?" Wu replied. "If they see me there with a foreigner, I'll be marked for life."

It took me a few weeks to convince her. Finally, we met in Majialou, in the southern part of the city. "My husband thinks I'm getting together with some friends on the faculty. If he finds out about what we're going to do, he'll kill me. I promised him I wouldn't go back to these places," she said as soon as she arrived. She had brought several reports along with her, and she wanted to explain to me how the sex towns had evolved in recent years. We sat down to have something to drink. With a paper and pen, Wu drew out some charts and pictures as we sipped some sour prune juice.[6]

"When I started researching this phenomenon in 2005, there were around a hundred of these places in Beijing, always around construction sites. The migrants who had left their families in the countryside needed to have sex once in a while. The prostitutes recognized an opportunity there. They started building little shacks around the barracks where the workers slept. They were really small, about fifty or sixty square feet, without electricity or running water, just with a table and a mattress. The girls charged between 50 and 100 yuan (eight to fifteen dollars). They turned into little towns when some lazy men who didn't want to work at construction realized they could make money off of these girls, and they offered them protection. They started to bring their neighbors, their sisters, daughters and wives from their villages in the country. They built the little shacks for the prostitutes to have sex with their clients, and they took a commission of 20 or 30 yuan (four or five dollars) for each time. Then those places started to get dangerous," Wu told me.

"How many sex towns are left now?" I asked, pouring her more juice.

"I'd say that before the Olympic Games in 2008, there were around a hundred. But the government carried out a major clean-up operation throughout the city: no prostitutes or beggars could be in any area where tourists might see them. They demolished many settlements. Now there are around twenty or thirty left, scattered between downtown and the outskirts of the city. With all the real estate development going on, there are construction sites even around the sixth ring,[7] and those kinds of prostitutes go wherever the workers are."

Wu wanted to show me one of the more notorious sex towns, between the fourth and fifth road ringing the city, which the police largely ignored because some officials were clients of the prostitutes there. The metro didn't go there, and it was too risky to take a bus: if a foreigner got off at that bus stop, it was easy to assume they were a journalist. Our best bet, Wu said, was to take a gypsy cab.

"If driver ask, you no talk," Wu murmured in her rudimentary English, as we got in the taxi. The driver, a young man who couldn't have been more than twenty, was munching on a sausage on a stick. He offered us a bite with a smile, and Wu politely refused. He finished the sausage in two bites, and opened up a bottle of sweet green tea. The driver's seat was fully reclined, and he had a crudely executed homemade tattoo on his wrist.

"I'll put some music on for you," he said, turning on the radio. The backseat began to vibrate from the rumbling bass notes of the techno music. Wu was sweating, and tried to open her window, but it was broken.

"Are you hot? A pretty girl like you can't be hot in my car," he said, and opened the two backseat windows. He was driving so fast that we were hit by a sudden blast of air, and I thought we might fly out of the car. He chatted away, trying to impress Wu, who couldn't wait to get out of the cab.

He dropped us off near the university, and wanted to wait with us until the friend we were supposedly meeting arrived. Wu managed to send him on his way after she scribbled down a phone number on a piece of paper and gave it to him; she told me later she had given him a wrong number.

Garbage was piled up by the entrance to the makeshift settlement, located right beside the police station. An elderly woman squatted down, picking through a mound of rotten food scraps, newspapers and household electronics that had been thrown in the trash. The public toilets were right at the entrance too, consisting of a brick shed with no door, with two stalls inside separated by a small wall. The combined stench rising from the garbage and the latrines was unbearable. On one side of the toilet shed someone had scrawled the character for "man", and the character for "woman" on the other. Both latrines emptied out into a foul stream running along the sides of the brick walls. Raw human waste, cigarette butts and flies flowed along the disgusting canal. Unsurprisingly, there was no drainage system, typical of areas of China outside of the central cities. One thing that did stand out were the hundreds of fliers tacked up on the walls, advertising abortion clinics and treatments for sexually transmitted diseases.

To get into the neighborhood, first the revolting stream emanating from the toilets had to be crossed. It had rained the day before, and the unpaved ground was muddy. It could have been any little street in any of the poorest neighborhoods in Beijing, lined with tiny, uninsulated shacks, some of the residents cooking out in the street over a gas stove. There were several little stores selling everything from beer to detergent. One hand-drawn sign advertised a bowl of noodles for thirty cents. "Now keep your eyes open," Wu warned.

As we walked along, we came across clinics with doors made of white aluminum, like little prefab sheds. We passed by stores that sold unguents, roots and medicinal herbs for strengthening the immune system, preventing infections or increasing sexual stamina. Women stood around on corners, waiting for customers. They were mostly between forty and sixty years old, with theatrically applied makeup, their faces very pale, with eyebrows painted on, like opera singers.

There were only two restaurants, so we went into the one toward the end of the street to sit down and talk. It was three o'clock, too late for lunch and too early for dinner, so we had the place to ourselves. The owner sat lounging in a chair with a cat on her lap, a soap opera blaring loudly from the television. She grunted at us. Wu ordered a plate of sliced tomatoes with sugar, and a bottle of orangeade. After a while the owner reappeared, muttering, and set down the tomatoes and drink.

"Those women you saw outside are taking a huge risk, because no one has taught them how to protect themselves from AIDS," Wu explained. "Some of them don't even know what it is. They get shots of medicine, and they think that's enough to prevent everything."

The HIV virus is a major concern for the Chinese authorities. Some 780,000 people are living with the virus, but half of them do not even know it, according to the United Nations.[8] Every year 50,000 people are infected, particularly prostitutes, their customers, homosexuals who do not practice safe sex, and drug addicts who share needles. Experts acknowledge that the actual figures could be much higher, because there are many men who have been sleeping with prostitutes for half of their lives but have never had an AIDS test. In the poorest areas of China, over half of the sex workers do not use condoms, and many men believe that sexually transmitted diseases are no more serious than catching the flu.[9] It is estimated that between thirty and fifty million people are at high risk of contracting the virus.

I ask Wu how involved organized crime syndicates are in prostitution. After talking to prostitutes over the last fifteen years, Wu has concluded that 90% of them get into the profession of their own free will. They mostly choose to go into prostitution because they need the money, not because they were victims of a crime ring. "The typical Chinese prostitute is a woman who has worked other kinds of jobs. Did you know many of them were waitresses before, around some nightclub? They work in the restaurants where the prostitutes go out to dinner with their customers. The waitresses see how they live, and find out how much they make each month. They see that the sex workers are uglier than they are, but they wear nicer clothes, and they can afford to go out to dinner, because they make ten times more money. So they decide to become prostitutes too."

But the other ten percent go through living hell. They are the victims of human traffickers.[10] According to the All-China Women's Federation, traffickers exploit the fact that young people from rural areas want to migrate to the cities or the factories on the coast. They recruit them in their villages, promising them work in restaurants or in industry. Wu sadly describes how she has known many such victims. She has a special place in her heart for Meimei,[11] a girl from Sichuan who managed to escape from her traffickers after six years.

Meimei's story is horrifying. As a small girl, her family did not let her go to school. Her father wanted to send her to work as soon as possible. When she was just thirteen, he sent her to Beijing with a neighbor, who was supposedly going to get her a job as a waitress. Once they arrived in the capital, the seemingly friendly neighbor turned out to be a soulless criminal who trafficked adolescent virgins. He beat Meimei and held her captive. The girl spent several years in a nightclub working as a sex slave. She tried to escape twice but was caught. She did successfully get away on her third attempt, but since she was illiterate, she couldn't read the classified ads to see what other kinds of jobs were available. She started to work as a prostitute in the street to earn enough money to eat. When Wu saw her for the first time, Meimei was half-naked in a park, waiting for some man to approach her. She was twenty years old, but looked much older, with a glassy-eyed stare, her body covered with scars, and utterly defenseless. Wu took her out to have a bowl of soup, and over time, they became friends. Five years later, Meimei knows how to read and write many Chinese characters, and every six months she gets a medical checkup. She has suffered severe psychological damage from her ordeal, and still has not been able to find another kind of work.

As Wu tells me Meimei's sad story, several customers come into the restaurant. A grandmother with her grandson orders some soup, and two men sit down at the table next to ours. When Wu looks over at them, she grows pale. She says it's getting late and quickly gets the check.

In the taxi back downtown, Wu tells me it's better not to stick around too long in those areas. The men could have been cops, or pimps. "Once, when I was doing research for my thesis, I went to a neighborhood like that on the outskirts of the city, and took some pictures. A man told me that if I didn't delete them, he would break my camera. He got really aggressive, I had to delete the pictures right in front of him so he would let me go. Ever since then, I'm more cautious," she explained.

The pimps don't like curious onlookers. And with their long history of abusing sex workers, the police don't like any extra attention, either. For years, the government would publicize their operations combating prostitution by parading prostitutes through the streets to humiliate them. They were known as "walks of shame," a kind of exercise in public ridicule typical of the Cultural Revolution. In 2006, one hundred sex workers from Canton had to endure a collective shaming, as they were shouted at and booed, an event that was broadcast on television. In another government action, dozens of names and addresses of prostitutes and their customers were posted on the Internet. But most Web surfers do not approve of these campaigns. In July 2010, photos of two young sex workers, barefoot, handcuffed and tied, generated a barrage of criticism. People who saw the photos on the Internet condemned the harsh treatment and lack of empathy toward these two girls who had not hurt anyone, and wondered why corrupt public officials were not chastised in the same manner.

The government responded by banning the walks of shame. According to Wu, the punishment was still practiced, but on a smaller scale. She will never forget a night in 2007, when several of her prostitute friends called her up, crying tears of rage. Some police officers had doused them with ice water and had made them stand outside in the street for hours, in the middle of winter, just to humiliate them. One of the women who had confronted the officers in defense of the sex workers was Mrs. Zhen.

Wu had promised her friend that she wouldn't leave Beijing before seeing her. After our excursion to the sex district, we go to Zhen's house. The two women grasp hands and gaze at each other affectionately.

"How pretty you are, motherhood becomes you," Zhen says, pinching Wu's cheeks.

"Come on, I'm so fat!" Wu replies with a laugh. She looks around the living room. "You're place looks lovely, big sister![12] And this?" she points to a four-foot-tall portrait of Zhen, all made up with her hair done, holding a bouquet of orchids, looking like a movie star.

"That photo was taken of me last year. I was out with some friends, and we came across a new photo studio that was having a promotion. They did our make-up and hair for 30 yuan ($4.80). It's not bad, right?"

She serves us tea and a dish of dried fruit, and turns on the fan. She remarks she's beginning to experience hot flashes, a symptom of menopause. They talk about work, Wu's new baby, and how hot the summer has been.

Wu asks how she's doing. Zhen explains she's been feeling tired, since she's not twenty years old anymore, but that being an old hand has its advantages: the police have not bothered her in quite a while. When an important date approaches, like the anniversary of the Communist Party, the police round up sex workers in the clubs, fine them, and throw a few of them and their pimps in jail to serve as an example. But after that, everything returns to normal.

She's anxious for the New Year holiday. It's her only vacation, and she'll take a month off to go back to her village. She spends time with her siblings, watching television, playing cards, setting off firecrackers, and cooking all day long. She's most anxious to see her son.

"How are things with him?" Wu asks carefully. She knows it's a touchy subject for her friend.

"The same as always. The problem with my son is he doesn't know what I have gone through, so he doesn't understand me. I hope he gets married soon. I don't think he has a girlfriend yet."

"Aren't you going to introduce him to someone?"

"No, he wouldn't let me. He can choose, as long as he has children soon," Zhen says. Wu nods sympathetically.

That is Mrs. Zhen's dream: to pack up her suitcase when her grandson is born and go back to her village, leaving behind the life in Beijing that her family knows nothing about, and focus on being a grandmother.

9

⧫⧫⧫⧫⧫

Beijing, Seen from a Taxi

Zhang Xiaodong wipes the taxi's windshield with his jacket sleeve. He had been asleep for two hours, and the vapor from his breath has fogged up the windows. The air is heavy and smells of garlic. He rolls down the window and a fresh breeze rushes in. He cracks his knuckles, turns his head back and forth to loosen up his neck, and steps out of the car to stretch his legs.

Dozens of cabs are lined up in a row behind him. The drivers are still sleeping, their seats reclined, their feet resting on the dashboards. At fifty-eight, Zhang Xiaodong can't sleep like that anymore. He lights a cigarette, wipes the morning dew off the front of his car and sits down in front of the canal that runs beside the road. Two city workers go up and down the canal in a little boat, fishing algae and trash out of the green water with nets. The highway is on the other side. When the sun comes up, the noise from the traffic will be deafening, but at the moment you can only hear the chirping of the birds, and the low hum of the boat's motor.

He is only halfway through his shift. He lives a two-hour drive outside of Beijing, and it didn't make sense to make the trip both ways each day. So instead he works for twenty hours straight, and then takes twenty hours off, to spend the least amount of money. He has it all calculated. The cost of renting the taxi, money for gas, and tolls are all accounted for. Since the price of gas has gone up (it costs double what it did just five years ago), he has to work much more to earn his 2,400 yuan ($378), the amount he needs to buy groceries and pay his wife's medical bills.

After a few stretches and a drink of tea from his thermos, he's ready to get back behind the wheel.

When he first started working as a driver back in 1986, cars in Beijing were a luxury reserved for wealthy business-men and the Party elite. Everyone else took the bus or got around on bicycles. The streets were always clear, no matter the time of day. Zhang Xiaodong remembers how much fun it was to drive along Jing Shan Avenue, speeding up and hitting the brakes whenever he liked, cruising by the Imperial Gardens and the For-bidden City's golden rooftops. King of the road, he could drive from one end of the city to the other in just twenty minutes.

Now it takes two hours to cover the same distance. Beijing's traffic is just as congested as in Mexico City or Sao Paulo. With five million vehicles,[1] traffic jams are commonplace. Chaos can erupt from any incident: a bus blocking a traffic light, several cars trying to beat a red light winding up trapped in the middle of the intersection . . . and the gridlock spreads out from there. Drivers vent their frustration by leaning on their horns, or getting out of their cars, ignoring the desperate pleadings of a traffic cop. There are hundreds of videos on the Internet, posted by residents who record the unruly scene from their windows, and comment on how horrible traffic conditions in the city have become.

Traffic is one of the most exasperating issues to Beijing's residents. They all remember the "world's biggest traffic jam," as the international press dubbed the event that took place in the summer of 2010. For more than ten days, the highway between Beijing and the Autonomous Region of Tibet became a trap because it was undergoing some construction work, and some accidents took place that blocked it completely. For sixty miles, thousands of vehicles were brought to a virtual standstill, creeping along at the maddening pace of as little as one mile per day. Resigned to their fate, drivers and their passengers slept, went out for little walks, and played cards. They had no other choice but to attend to their personal needs between the cars on the road. They only got really angry when, sensing a business opportunity, some of the locals living near the road started selling them water and instant noodles at four times the usual price.

The notorious highway pile-up put traffic at the epicenter of a debate in the media. Could a highway system constructed sixty years ago handle current truck traffic? the experts wondered. The government acknowledged that it could not. Keeping major cities like Beijing supplied with energy came at a price: the roads are oversaturated, and battered by high levels of truck traffic bringing in raw materials and merchandise. It is estimated that congestion on the highway where the world's biggest traffic jam happened has increased by 40% over just a few years, because central Mongolia is now the capital city's major source of coal.

Beijing's issues are a little different: car fever is strangling the city. The five major roadways that circumnavigate the metropolitan area boast smooth pavement that would be the envy of Rome or New York, but there are not enough lanes to accommodate all the traffic. Spurred on by economic incentives after the government decided the automotive sector had to experience strategic growth in order for them to complete with Germany,

Japan and the United States, consumers eagerly snapped up the ultimate status symbol. The time had come for China to get behind the wheel.

In 2009, entire families would visit car showrooms together. A salary of 5,000 yuan ($800) a month was enough to purchase a car priced in the midrange.[2] Families who could afford it bought two. Drivers in the countryside, who got credit for trading in their old vehicles, carefully inspected the new models over and over again, adjusting the rearview mirrors, and reclining the seats backward and forward. Aspiring drivers who hadn't saved up enough money yet lingered over the latest models on car dealers' lots, leaving with a photo of the one they planned to buy for themselves in the future.

Shanghai became the new Detroit. And China became the world's biggest market for automobiles, eclipsing the United States. In 2010, eighteen million vehicles were sold. To many analysts, things were moving too fast. In terms of cars per capita, China still lagged far behind other developed nations,[3] but the cities were unprepared for the sudden car craze. The Transportation Research Center published reports finding that traffic in Beijing was moving at slower and slower speeds, and that congestion could reach alarming levels by 2015.

The government hit the brakes. It stopped providing financial incentives, and in late 2010 formally restricted the number of new car registrations.[4] Many people resorted to the black market or called on their contacts to get their car registered anyway, but the formal restrictions and the higher price of gas resulted in declining sales.[5] Measures were taken to reduce congestion and pollution levels. Electric cars were actively promoted, and improvements were made to public transportation and the subway system, one of the biggest in the world. And cars were only allowed to drive on alternate days, according to the final digit of the license plate.

In spite of these measures, Zhang Xiaodong estimates that he spends about three hours stuck in traffic every day. And that's driving him to despair. To earn 520 yuan ($83), he needs to work shifts that are at least twelve hours long. When the car isn't moving, the meter runs more slowly, and his earnings are cut in half. He stared at the barely moving odometer helplessly, worrying over how much money he would lose.

Music helps to calm his attacks of nerves. He listens to everything, except for techno: Chinese opera, Mozart, Bruce Springsteen, local rock bands. Shortly after we met, he gave me a CD by Dao Lang, his favorite folk singer, from the Sichuan province. "My daughter recorded it. She's my modern music professor," he said, putting the CD into his taxi's stereo system. He knew all the words:

> *The first snowfall of 2002*
> *Brings me a sad story in Urumqi,[6] that I can't forget*
> *You were like a butterfly fluttering its wings*
> *Over the virgin snow, like a sparkling flame.*

He crooned the verses in his raspy voice of a lifelong smoker. "I have listened to this record a thousand times. And I like the radio, but music fills up more space. It keeps me company. While I sing, I don't think about things so much. The hours go by very slowly behind the wheel."

He had bright black eyes, and a weather-beaten, tanned complexion, with fine, white lines etched into his face. When he smiled, he exposed crooked, stained teeth, and a metallic glint from a poorly fitting bridge. Like many Chinese men, he had a long fingernail on his pinky, just under an inch. This was a kind of status symbol, because it meant he didn't do manual labor. The men use it like a Swiss army knife: to scratch an itch, dig wax out of their ears, pick their noses, open packages, separate bills and, in Zhang Xiaodong's case, to fiddle with during traffic jams.

From his vantage point, Zhang has seen how the large town that Beijing once was had become a breathtaking city. When the civil war ended in 1949 and the People's Republic was declared in Tiananmen Square, there were barely any buildings over two stories high. Sixty years later, the skyline features towering skyscrapers designed to resemble torches, can openers and spirals. This is the new Beijing, many Western architects' dream, where everything is possible.

The sour note in this epic transformation is all the buildings of historical significance that have been destroyed along the way. The value of the structures that have been lost since Mao's regime is incalculable. Wang Jun, a journalist specializing in urban issues and author of *Cheng Ji* (城记), a bestseller on Beijing's evolution, has painstakingly documented the demolitions. One of the most symbolic took place in 1954, when Maoists destroyed the Temple of Celebrating Longevity. Built in the twelfth century, it was one of the city's jewels. The Mongols respected the temple when they took over Beijing as their capital.[7] The Communist Party's engineers had other priorities, and were determined to draw a straight line from east to west right through the city no matter the cost. The Avenue of Heavenly Peace now crosses over where the renowned Buddhist temple once stood.

The destruction peaked during the Cultural Revolution (1966–1976). The Red Guard, young paramilitaries blindly devoted to the cult of Mao, were given orders to destroy all symbols of the past, and rebuild the country from the ground up. With the government cheering them on, they reduced thousands of centuries-old buildings to ashes. They sacked museums, temples and *si-heyuan*, the emblematic Pekinese homes made of gray brick with tile roofs.[8] The owners of these dwellings had whatever they could shipped abroad, or hid parts of it. Still, countless wooden doors intricately carved by hand, handcrafted antiques, furniture, tapestries, and centuries of precious history were lost.

With the economic liberalization of 1978, the new mantra became growth, growth, growth. The middle class had to be strengthened, and tall buildings and shopping centers had to be built for them and the thousands of migrants arriving from the countryside. Entire neighborhoods of single-story houses were bulldozed. Hundreds of thousands of dwellings were expropriated, their owners cast out of the city center, and relocated to far-flung neighborhoods on the outskirts. Real estate boomed, becoming one of the most lucrative, and most unsettled, sectors of the economy.[9]

Three decades later, twenty-two million people live in Beijing, and the map keeps on changing. Over the course of just a few weeks, an entire block of houses can disappear. In the driver's seat, Zhang Xiaodong has to keep complicated mental notes on the best routes to take in his head, so he won't get lost, and to avoid streets blocked by construction. When he's feeling nostalgic, he drives along the old wall's ruins. Few people know that for almost five hundred years, from 1435 up until 1965, the capital of China was fortified by a fifty-foot wall, almost fifteen miles long, with nine entrances. Mao Zedong ordered it demolished to make way for construction of the city's first highway, the so-called second ring, and the first line of the metro. Many experts were horrified by this decision, but there was nothing they could do.[10] The only part of the wall still intact is a pair of doors that stand alone next to the highway[11] and a small section of wall overtaken by weeds near the south train station. People go there to walk their dogs.

We had gone to see the ruins of the wall, and suddenly felt hungry. We parked the taxi just outside a *hutong*, a labyrinth of old traditional little streets, in search of some good home-style cooking. Near the constant roar of the highway, the *hutongs* are surprisingly silent, like an oasis in the desert. The neighborhood is made up of low houses and vegetable stands. People get around on bicycles, everyone knows everyone else, and the children can safely play outside on their own. He Suzhong, founder of the Center for the Protection of Cultural Heritage, always says that if he had to choose a place that best represented traditional Chinese culture, it would be a *hutong*. It embodies a whole way of life.

But if you want to appreciate the area's unique charms, you'd better hurry. "This street won't be around for much longer," Zhang Xiaodong said, gesturing to a row of humble homes that had been thrown together from cheap materials, with no heat or running water. Many of them were real hovels. The character 拆 (*chai*) had been painted in white on several front doors: it meant they were marked for demolition. We counted eight of them.

On one corner, two women washed their hair in a basin. A small boy who was just learning to walk toddled after a hen, which hurried ahead, trying to evade its pursuer, shedding tail feathers in its wake. The aroma of lamb wafted onto the street from the back kitchen door of a Muslim restaurant. A cook wearing a filthy apron opened the door to throw some leftover food onto a pile of rubbish rotting in a corner.

At the end of the street we saw a tangle of bicycles and *sanlunche*, the big three-wheeled bikes used as Pedicabs or by vendors to carry merchandise. "If so many people are parked there, there must be someplace with great food," Zhang Xiaodong observed, and quickened his step, as if he had just caught the scent of something. He wasn't wrong: as we rounded the corner, we saw a ramshackle little restaurant, packed with customers. The whole place was barely fifty square feet, with prefab walls, and no bathroom (people use communal toilets in the *hutongs*). The owners of the modest establishment had improvised an outdoor patio with folding tables and little stools, just six inches off the ground. You had to practically squat down to sit on them, a position that the Chinese generally find very comfortable. We both ordered the *dan dan mian*, Sichuan noodles in hot sauce, with pork, vegetables and scallions. Zhang Xiaodong added several cloves of garlic as a garnish. The Chinese rarely omit fresh garlic from meals, it's as common an accompaniment as bread in Western cuisine.

Three men wearing taxi driver uniforms at another table waved at us.

"Old man Zhang! You here for lunch?" Shouted a chubby man with a shaved head. He gestured for us to sit with them. Their names were Lu, Lao Wang and Xiao Lin. They had known each other for years, but rarely ran into each other because they worked different shifts. "We're celebrating, Lu's going to be a grandfather!" exclaimed Xiao Lin, the one with the shaved head. They had the waiter bring over two more glasses, and poured us some rice liquor to toast their friend. We pushed our two tables together. "How wonderful, there's going to be a little dragon!"[12] exclaimed Zhang Xiaodong.

Lu and Xiao Lin worked for the same company as Zhang Xiaodong. They lived in Pingu and Miyun respectively, two towns outside of the capital, and also worked as many hours as possible each shift to save on gasoline. On the other hand, Lao Wang had lived in Beijing his whole life, and worked from seven-thirty in the morning until four in the afternoon. He wasn't worried about making less money, because his wife worked as a nurse in a good hospital. "She's the boss, she earns more than I do, so I have to do more of the housework," he said with a laugh. "Driving a taxi in Beijing isn't a good business anymore."

The three were working the same shift that day, and decided to take a few hours off for lunch, taking advantage of the parking lot the second ring roadway had turned into because of an accident. "I bet fifty yuan one of the cars that crashed is some rich guy's Mercedes," Xiao Lin joked. "They buy the most expensive cars, and they don't even know how to drive," he laughed. "Then the other car better be a gypsy cab," Mr. Lu said wryly. Of the one hundred thousand taxis in Beijing, approximately thirty thousand are *hei che* ("black cars"), cars of private citizens who made their living driving people around the city. Mr. Lu, who dyed his carefully styled hair black, hated them because he thought they cut into his business. Zhang Xiaodong forgave them: "The *hei che* are just trying to get by. This city is getting more and more expensive, and they have a rough life. When I drive down a street and I see them parked waiting for customers, I just go down the other side and that's it."

The way Zhang Xiaodong sees it, his coworkers are just wasting their energy railing against the unauthorized gypsy cab drivers, instead of standing up to their employers. He never raised his voice, but his jugular vein popped out when he talked about his company's owners: "They're swine, real pigs who fritter away the money we're not making," he exclaimed. In all of China, there are 8,700 taxi companies which employ some two million drivers.[13]

As the bottle of rice liquor quickly disappeared, the drivers explained that each company operated independently in its own way, with one thing in common: they all bled their employees dry. "At mine, every month they have two incredibly boring meetings to talk about traffic rules, safety and how to treat customers," Zhang Xiaodong complained. "We are required to attend. Right before when the meeting is supposed to start, they turn off our meters by remote control, so that we can't keep on working. We lose half a day. And no one makes up that lost money for us. The cost to rent the taxi is the same." His colleagues nodded.

"The proof that we're just clowns to them is this ridiculous uniform, just look at it," Xiao Lin exclaimed, grabbing the shirt he has had to wear ever since the Olympic Games. A month before, in July 2008, a municipal order was issued, requiring all the taxi companies to provide uniforms to their employees. It was China's debut on the world stage, and the Government wanted to make a good impression. Spitting, eating garlic (so they wouldn't have bad breath) and smoking were all forbidden in the taxis. Zhang Xiaodong and his colleagues could get away with disobeying those rules, but there was no way around the uniform. They were issued two pairs of navy blue pants, a yellow shirt, and a tie with black and yellow stripes. The fine for refusing to wear the uniform was 200 yuan. "You don't know how itchy this thing is. There's no cotton. It's a cheap material. When I sweat, it's unbearable," Xiao Lin protested, the shirt buttons over his belly about to pop after the big meal.

The sight of my recorder on the table loosened the tongues of the four drivers, encouraging them to air their grievances. "These pants and this shirt would cost 150 yuan ($23) at the most in the stores. We have two uniforms, so that's 300 yuan. The company deducted 800 from our paychecks. Isn't that just plain stealing?" Zhang Xiaodong insisted.

"The uniform doesn't bother me, but the inspections are killing me," Mr. Lu lamented. "They penalize us if our taxi is dirty, but they have never told us exactly what the standards of cleanliness are. They can fine me for a piece of hair in the backseat from some customer, for one little hair! In the end they just want money. And those thieves act out of personal vengeance. If your company isn't getting along with the police, they're much more strict, they look for the smallest excuse to fine us. If it's a small thing, you pay the fine, but if it's something that's going to cost a lot of money and you have to notify the company, you'll be left without a job," he explained.

Mr. Lu was obsessed with keeping his taxi clean, because just one sanction would mean he couldn't pay all his bills that month. He flatly refused to drive children, people in wheelchairs, or workers in dirty clothes in his cab. He cataloged his prejudices with surprising candor. "I don't like people from the northeast, not from any of the three provinces,"[14] he stated, cleaning his teeth with a toothpick and then sucking on it. "Whether they're men or women, they say too many vulgar things. There are good people too, but in general they have no education in the northeast. The Pekinese always call me 'driver' and then tell me the address. They get into the taxi and say, 'go straight' and point. They make me uncomfortable. I don't like the people from Xinjiang either. There are a lot of cheats and thieves in that province, they are uncivilized. They don't get along with us, we're ethnically Han."[15] And when it came to foreigners, he clarified that he did not like to drive Russians or Africans.

"I try to avoid driving down Yabao Lu," acknowledged Zhang Xiaodong, referring to the main street in Beijing's Russian neighborhood, "because I'm afraid I won't understand them when they talk." To him, the worst were the young people, foreigners and Chinese alike. "They're always drunk on the weekends, and get the directions wrong. A guy even got into my cab saying he didn't have any money but that I had to drive him anyway. I don't protest in those situations. I don't want any trouble. Once a guy stole my phone when I got out to buy cigarettes."

The woman who owned the restaurant came over and asked us if we wanted more rice liquor. "Of course we do, sister," Xiao Lin rubbed his belly, "but we have to get back to work. If I sit here anymore I'm going to fall asleep," he added, and slowly got to his feet.

In weeks when there wasn't much work, Xiao Lin didn't even go home. He slept in the taxi between the third ring highway and the Museum of Modern Art, on a quiet street where dozens of cab drivers like him had set up a base of operations. It was like a campsite. Each one had staked out a place to park, they washed out their clothes in the public bathroom and hung them to dry on a makeshift clothesline tied to two lamp posts. They could buy a hot meal at a food cart that was open all night, and the bars in the area let them fill up their thermoses with hot water for tea. If they couldn't sleep, there was always somebody else still awake who they could talk to.

Zhang Xiaodong had made the same sacrifices so he could work more hours, but he had to help his wife out tending the garden, and especially, he had to take care of her. When she had an attack of vertigo, she would spend days lying in bed, unable to move.

Zhang and his wife lived in a town at the foot of the mountains in Yanqing County, one of the two counties of Beijing, a two hour's drive from the city center. They lived in the same house Zhang had grown up in with his father and two sisters, with no bathroom or washing machine. His mother died when he was just six years old. They were dirt poor, as many were at the time. Zhang Xiaodong only attended five years of school, starting when he was nine until he was fourteen. He loved reading adventure stories and playing Ping-Pong. There was a Ping-Pong table at the school's playground, and he would spend hours playing with his friends. "I could have gone somewhere with that if I had really practiced, but it wasn't to be. I was really good," he remembered with a smile. In 1966 he left school, along with millions of other children. The Cultural Revolution had begun.

Taking advantage of a break during his shift, we met in Fuchengmen, a neighborhood in the western part of the city, on an avenue where seniors train their pet birds. Some birds are so well-trained, they seem like dogs. They can pick coins out of their owners' hands with their beaks, and respond to their whistles. Zhang told me he would have liked to have trained pigeons, a very typical Pekinese hobby banned during the Cultural Revolution. The absurd list of activities prohibited for "hindering the triumph of socialism" also included flying kites.

"It was a mistake to try and erase education and traditions," he asserted, as we walked under the willow trees. His memories of that decade are hazy. As soon as he left school, he began working as a delivery boy. "I remember a lot of chaos and unrest. Different Red Guard factions were always confronting everybody. I was just a boy, but I found it shocking to see people my own age insulting teachers."

The Red Guard were students, barely twenty years old, ignorant paramilitaries that president Mao mobilized to "fight against the bourgeoisie and elites."[16] Actually he used them to undermine another wing of the party, which Mao accused of being procapitalist, and to reinforce his own power base. He had them trained to rebel against their elders, something diametrically opposed to traditional Chinese mores. Zhang Xiaodong remembers how the Red Guard made his teachers parade around wearing cone-shaped paper hats, signs with insults written on them hanging from their necks, as they made the rest of the students boo and hiss at them. The official policy was to eliminate the *si jiu* (四旧), the four main ingredients of the past: "old customs, old ideas, old habits and old culture."[17] One of the propaganda posters of 1967 shows a young man destroying with a hammer a crucifix, a statue of the Buddha, and classic Chinese texts.

A perverse cult grew around Mao's image. In 1969, 2.2 billion badges emblazoned with Mao's face were sold.[18] Streets were renamed with "red" names. Temples and museums were sacked. Students and professionals were exiled from the cities and sent out to the countryside to learn from the peasants.[19] Writers, philosophers and teachers had to collect excrement from the public latrines as part of their "reeducation". The Government detained many people in forced labor camps, or relocated families off of their land to remote provinces. Killings, torture and rape were committed and tolerated by the authorities. Millions died, and the suicide rate skyrocketed.[20]

In some cases atrocities committed went beyond all imaginable limits: in the southern province of Guangxi, cases of cannibalism were documented. The Red Guards killed, butchered, cooked and ate several school principals to celebrate the triumph of the revolution. Human corpses were on display in dining rooms, hung from hooks as if they were livestock. The writer Zheng Yi, one of the most-hunted dissidents because of his participation in the Tiananmen protests, asserts that at least 137 people were executed and eaten in this way in the late sixties. There is no evidence that Mao was aware of what was happening, but there is proof that several local leaders instigated the depraved acts and covered them up.[21] It is perhaps the case of cannibalism with the most number of active participants in the twentieth century: thousands of people took part in these bloody banquets to demonstrate their loyalty to the Communist Party.

The collective paranoia subsided in 1969, but the Cultural Revolution did not draw to a close until seven years later, when Mao died. Gradually, the country as a whole began to lift itself up, in spite of the fact that its economy was in ruins.[22]Millions of shattered lives were reassembled. In 1977, the universities opened their doors once again, and intellectuals were reinserted into public life. Young people who had been shipped out to the country to learn from the farmers and rural peasants could finally return home to their families. A decade of panic seared into China's collective memory, inspiring intense curiosity in experts in mass psychology, had finally ended.

For Zhang Xiaodong's family, their grinding poverty was their salvation. His father was illiterate, and the three children barely had ten years of combined schooling between them. "They treated us well because we were workers, and supposedly we had to rule the country, but they imposed a lot of rules on us. For example, we couldn't cook at home, because the kitchens were collective. This was fine for us because we barely had anything to eat, but now that I think about it, we didn't have any other choice. It was a hard time." Even the most devout Maoists acknowledge it. Over the years, many members of the Red Guard, overcome with guilt, have become the most strident critics of the Cultural Revolution.[23]

As we waited for the traffic congestion to abate somewhat, we sat on a bench to watch the older people playing with their sparrows. Zhang Xiaodong had to be back on the highway by seven that evening. I asked him if he had ever heard of an article titled, "After Forty-four Years, the Red Guard Start to Apologize," that had made such a strong impact on public opinion in China when it was published in November 2010. It was the first report on the subject to appear in continental China,[24] and it was published by *Nanfang Zhoumo*, one of the few semi-independent daily newspapers. "Yes, I heard something about that on the radio," he replied. "Maybe in other countries it would be hard to understand, but in China, almost all the victims want to forgive and forget. Why stir up the past again. We have so many new problems, we can't worry about the old ones." He lit a cigarette, and slowly exhaled the smoke through his nose.

In spite of everything, Zhang Xiaodong considers himself a Maoist. In his wallet, he carries a red stamp with a picture of the Great Helmsman. "Chairman Mao took care of the Chinese people, and gave them their honor back," he exclaimed effusively, showing me the stamp. He believes that people like him owed their lives to Mao for having sent doctors into the countryside. Before 1949, the smallest epidemic would take thousands of lives. Mao, who made fun of the Ministry of Health for being elitist (he called it the "Ministry of health for urban dwellers"[25]), instituted a program of rural doctors to bring basic medical attention to the villages, where 80% of the population lived. Millions of young people were selected to receive a basic medical education. They learned how to administer vaccines, bandage broken limbs and prevent infections, among other things. They were known as "barefoot doctors" (*chijiao yisheng*, 赤脚 医生) because, just like the rural peasants, many had no shoes.

After 1977, free basic medical care disappeared with the economic reforms, and everyone had to start paying for doctor's visits. A serious illness meant financial ruin. Zhang Xiaodong came down with tuberculosis, and had to ask his sister to lend him money to pay for his treatment. "I still haven't paid it all back. Fortunately that's what family is for," he says heavily. Many foreigners have a hard time comprehending that health care and education in China are privatized. Wasn't it a communist country? They wonder. Zhang Xiaodong wonders about this too.

The government embarked on a major health care reform initiative in 2009. By 2020, "China will have a basic health care system that can provide safe, effective, convenient and affordable health services to urban and rural residents," according to a statement from the official Xinhua news agency. The idea is that as a country they would become a *xiaokang shehui* (小康社会),[26] "moderately well-off society" or, literally, a society of small peace, comfort and health (peace is essential for the Communist Party, which wants to avoid instability at all costs.) But as long as people continue to set money aside instead of spending it, for fear of being struck by a medical emergency, there will be no way to stimulate the consumer economy.[27] The government spent 200 billion dollars in just the first two years of the initiative. Hospitals and rural health clinics received aid to buy equipment and to provide basic healthcare coverage to 90% of the population.[28]

In spite of the progress that has been made, healthcare remains far from universal. A great many patients cannot even afford the insurance co-payments; and migrant workers from the countryside are not covered in the cities. Public hospitals are still financed by the sale of medicines and drugs, which Zhang Xiaodong finds outrageous. The more drugs they prescribe, the more money they make. Abuse of the system is widespread, and the authorities acknowledge it. In some hospitals, the prices of medications are posted on giant electronic boards, like share prices on the stock exchange.

Zhang Xiaodong is convinced that Mao would have preserved free healthcare. "The Party is always saying the standard of living in China has gotten much better over the last thirty years. That's true. But, what about the inequality? Hasn't that gotten worse? If the poor get a serious illness, we die. If I got sick tomorrow, the treatment would cost between 200,000 and 300,000 yuan ($32,000–$47,000). The government would cover 40%, so I would have to pay 180,000 yuan ($29,000). I couldn't even scrape together $10,000. What would I do, financially ruin my family? I could never do that."

His top priority was to never be a burden to his two children, a daughter, 32, and a son, 28. They both worked at the prison in Tianjin, an industrial city about sixty miles from Beijing. "My daughter attended a Police Academy and got a job right after at the Department of Propaganda. Then she helped my son to get in. I don't like having them work there, especially her. She's in the offices, but sometimes she has to go into the prison part, and that's dangerous. I don't want anything to happen to her." He saw his son, who's still single, every weekend. He saw his married daughter less often, because she lives far away, but she had given him the greatest joy of his life: a granddaughter.

She was five years old, and had her grandfather wrapped around her little finger. Everyone called her Ying Tao, Cherry, because she was born on April 28, and her grandfather brought a basket of ripe cherries to the hospital as a gift. "She's so smart," Zhang Xiaodong remarked with a bright smile that wiped the fatigue off his face. He saw her every two or three months, whenever he could take a few days off. "That's the happiest time of my life. My wife and I take her to the park and buy her a little toy, we go out to eat at a restaurant, we watch her play." He could go without eating to save a little money, but the visits to Cherry were sacred. He was thinking of bringing her a cricket as a surprise on his next visit. "When I was little I had many *guo guo*.[29] I loved catching bugs to feed to them, and to put them on the window sill so they would chirp even louder." He would buy his granddaughter a *guo guo* at the animal market and put it in a pink jar, Cherry's favorite color.

He had already started making plans for when he retires. He didn't know when that would be exactly, but he liked to think about it: he would plant chestnut trees in front of his house; he'd go to bed at nine o'clock every night, and sleep lying flat to ease his back pains. If he managed to save up enough money, he'd go on his dream vacation: a trip to Pyongyang. He had never left China, and wasn't interested in visiting other countries, except for North Korea. He was convinced he would find Beijing circa 1960 there. "I've seen it on television, the North Korean state looks after its people. Healthcare and education are free. It's a truly socialist country."

Packaged tours to North Korea have become very popular among the Chinese. To those who got all of their news from the official CCTV network (which is to say, the vast majority of the urban population and practically everyone in rural areas who owned a television), going to Pyongyang is a nostalgic trip back in time. Chinese propaganda paints a glowing picture of the Hermit Kingdom. Zhang Xiaodong had never in his life heard anything about the chronic famines and starvation, or the atrocities committed under Kim Jong Il.[30] "You can take a train there, and when you get to the border with South Korea, they let us Chinese get a few feet closer than any other foreigners,"[31] he pointed out dreamily.

Saving up enough money for the trip would not be easy, but he needed to have a goal. He was terrified at the thought of retiring and collecting a monthly pension of just 1,500 yuan ($235). How could he pay for his wife's medicines on that? And what if he got sick? "I could have gone into business, but I wouldn't have been any good at it. For a while I sold vegetables in Beijing. I brought them in from town and put them in the trunk of the car, but I would run into people I knew and they'd ask me for discounts. I didn't want to offend anyone, so I never said no, and I ended up losing a lot of money. My wife was furious," he remembered with a laugh. "Right now this is all I know how to do, and I have to keep doing it."

He had dropped off a fare near the Olympic village, and we met there. We were in the shadow of the Bird's Nest, the stadium where China grandly hosted the Olympic Games in 2008. We bought some *jiangbing*, a thin, fried egg pancake stuffed with vegetables and tofu, from a woman who prepared them to order, and we sat outside to watch the sunset.

He told me that Lu and Xiao Lin, the taxi drivers we had had lunch with, had gone on strike that week along with thousands of other drivers to demand better working conditions. Zhang Xiaodong didn't dare. He didn't expect that things would ever improve, and he was afraid of what his bosses would do. "What good does it do to ask the government to help us? There are thousands of businesses, the authorities can't worry about all of them. There's too much corruption. There's nothing you can do," he sighed. He seemed troubled. "I don't know. I talk to a lot of customers. Beijing is more developed than ever. We've never been able to buy so many things before. But I don't think my children could get rich. If you don't have money or contacts, no one helps you. The politicians' children are the ones who get the good jobs. Children of common people like me don't. The next generation of Chinese politicians will be the children of the current leaders. And we poor people will still be the slaves."

Did he think that wouldn't have been the case under Mao? I asked. Because even back then corruption had reached outrageous levels. "That's true. I think the political system in China is good, but corruption is a big problem. Still, the people don't complain much; we Chinese rarely criticize the government. We don't want any trouble. People are afraid they'll be thrown in jail or their children could pay the price," he explained.

But, I countered, in private most people talked about politics and criticized the Party's rampant corruption and nepotism. I had talked about politics many times myself with other taxi drivers. I had come across all types: those who were devoted to the Party, cynics, radicals, nihilists, perverts, romantics, and almost all of them liked to talk. Didn't he talk openly with his customers?

He started to laugh, and then coughed. He spit forcefully before answering.

"You foreigners are so nosy! Every person is different. I talk about politics with other drivers I know, but with customers, no."

Then what did he talk about?

"You'd be surprised what you can learn from strangers. I've

met lots of real characters in Beijing over the years. There are some really weird people out there. Women who ask me if their makeup looks alright, because they're going on a date . . . How should I know if their makeup is right? The other day a young woman got in the cab, I think she was a prostitute or dancer at a karaoke bar. She started to talk a mile a minute. She told me she had a new boyfriend from Henan, that he was a few years younger than her, and she didn't trust him. This girl said to me, 'Mr. Driver, do you think men from Henan are good people? I've heard they're liars.' She started to complain that this guy had asked her to marry him, but he didn't care about her enough. I think she was a little neurotic. I dropped her off at a banquet hall."

10

✦✦✦✦✦

The Dark Side of China

It was March 2008, and the phones were ringing off the hook at the office of one of the biggest foreign television networks in Beijing.[1] Linda, the lone Chinese staffer, had to answer all the calls. The first time she picked up the phone, she was shocked to hear the angry tirade spewing from the other end. "Lying bastards!" screeched a furious voice before hanging up. Hundreds of people called to complain about the network's coverage of the unrest in Tibet. One caller even threatened the lives of the reporters. It was a nightmare for Linda, who had only been working there for two weeks. Once they realized she was Chinese too, her fellow countrymen called her a traitor. "How can you work for the enemy?" they demanded.

High up in the Himalayas, Llasa, the Tibetan capital, was a battlefield at the time, rocked by the worst escalation of violence to occur over the past twenty years. Hundreds of Tibetans protested against what they viewed as China's cultural and religious oppression, exactly forty-nine years after the failed rebellion against Beijing took place in 1959. The flashpoint came when the Chinese police killed four Tibetan monks, according to the organization Free Tibet.[2] A group of Tibetans lashed out against their Han neighbors (the ethnic majority group in China), killing several, and set government buildings, stores and vehicles on fire. Terrified, many Han business owners fled the city. Beijing reacted by sending tens of thousands of troops to the region. According to Tibetan sources in exile and Amnesty International, the Chinese troops took over Llasa, firing rounds of real ammunition. They conducted a house-to-house search, looking for anyone who had participated in the unrest. They detained everyone who had a portrait of the Dalai Lama in their homes, and hundreds of Tibetans disappeared, according to Amnesty International. The protests and reprisals spread out to surrounding provinces with Tibetan communities. The secretary of the Communist Party in Tibet, Zhang Qingli, declared: "We are engaged in a fierce battle of blood and fire against the Dalai clique, a life-and-death struggle between the foe and us."

When she saw the first images of the unrest, Linda could not believe it. Pent-up frustration had been building up for years among Tibetans, but like many of her fellow Han, it didn't seem real to her until the violent protests erupted. The official media outlets did not show the monks' suicides, or make any mention of the everyday citizens who set themselves on fire to show their desperation.

A historic event was unfolding. It was another instance that clearly, shockingly illustrated just what a seething pressure cooker China was, but the international media could only cover it from a distance. It was impossible to enter Llasa, and the clamp-down had extended to surrounding provinces.[3] Foreign journalists gritted their teeth and cited conflicting reports from other sources, with no way to verify them. Tibetans in exile talked about gunfire, indiscriminate arrests, and massive round-ups conducted by Chinese troops. Beijing placed the blame for the bloodbath squarely on the shoulders of violent Tibetans. State authorities asserted that the Dalai Lama had instigated the protests to disrupt the Olympic Games that Beijing would host in August.

Several foreign media outlets mistakenly identified images of police beating Tibetan monks as having occurred in China, when those incidents in fact had happened in Nepal or India. Although some outlets apologized,[4] Beijing seized the opportunity to accuse the Western media of being biased in favor of Tibetans. According to official propaganda, the West wanted to slow China's progress, and tarnish their image in anticipation of the Olympic Games. This turbulent atmosphere prompted many Chinese to pick up the phone and, indignant, call Linda's office and give the network she worked for a piece of their minds.

Few issues do more damage to China's image abroad than the situation in Tibet, an autonomous region[5] with very strong nationalist sentiment and its own language, ethnicity, culture and religion. To Beijing, Tibet has been a part of China ever since the thirteenth century, when both were conquered by the Mongols. Tibetans dispute this version, and historical events support arguments on both sides. Up until the twentieth century, the region was more or less in line with the Chinese government, and, between 1913 and 1915, enjoyed a kind of de facto independence. After defeating the nationalists from Kuomintang in the civil war, Mao Zedong sent the People's Liberation Army into Tibet to take control of the region. In 1951 Mao reached an agreement with the Dalai Lama, the highest Tibetan authority, who did not oppose China's sovereignty. But relations deteriorated, culminating in the failed Tibetan uprising against China in 1959, and the subsequent self-imposed exile of the Dalai Lama.[6] Today he lives in Dharamsala, India, where he leads Tibet's government in exile.

From there, he demands autonomy for Tibet, but not complete independence or secession from China. The newest generation of Tibetan nationalists, especially those living abroad, are the ones demanding outright independence.

Beijing maintains that they liberated the Tibetan people from crushing poverty and freed them from being the vassals of feudal lords. Chinese authorities assert they have improved life expectancies in the region, and have strengthened health care and infrastructure. In recent decades, they have invested billions of dollars to build roads, providing access to one of the most inaccessible places on the planet, and a railroad line that can make the journey from Beijing to Lhasa (2,500 miles) in 48 hours. To Tibetans in exile, those capital investments, far from being altruistic, are textbook examples of colonialism. They insist Beijing has actively encouraged the emigration of ethnic Han to the region, relegating Tibetans to second-class status. Today, the Han dominate the economy in Tibet. The Chinese Communist Party keeps the region under strict control: thousands of soldiers are stationed there, foreign journalists are not allowed to enter the region unless they are on official, supervised visits, and the Party monitors Tibetan monks, journalists, bloggers and writers. Some are currently in prison for having sent information abroad. The International Federation for Human Rights talks about "systemic, flagrant violations of human rights and basic liberties" on Beijing's part. Hundreds of people have been forced to attend indoctrination sessions in retaliation after traveling to India to take classes with the Dalai Lama.

To Linda, the young Chinese journalist, she was struck by how much hatred was festering within her fellow countrymen. "I realized that Chinese people are in bad shape. They have a hard life and are deeply unhappy. If hypothetically we had made a mistake, the viewers could call and complain, but not make death threats.

It's a completely disproportionate reaction. Those calls were an excuse to vent their frustrations. I thought that something must be seriously wrong with Chinese society if people had all of that bottled up inside."

What was most striking to her was that the people who called and made threats could not have even seen the television station she worked for. First of all, they didn't speak English. And secondly, how could they have seen their coverage of Tibet, if the station had been censured inside of China? This meant that the unrest in Tibet had reached a whole other level. The official propaganda had stirred up patriotic fervor. The *fengqin*,[7] young nationalists (literally, "angry youth"), fill up Internet forums with harangues against the Western media and references to a colonial past. China has to rise up, they say.

A small percentage of the enraged *fengqin* did know English, and had followed the international media's coverage of the unrest in Tibet on the Internet. Some of Linda's friends were in this tiny group, who believed the West adopted positions based on their prejudices against Beijing. To them, it seems pathetic that Hollywood stars embrace the cause of the Tibetan people without ever mentioning the strategic interests that Russia, the United Kingdom, and the United States have historically had in the region, or that the CIA sent money to the Dalai Lama for years.

To some, it was the Tibetans' passive resistance and the fact that some self-immolated instead of throwing grenades that garnered strong support for their cause abroad. Beijing would never grant Tibet independence because it is a territory rich in natural resources, in a strategic geographic location. Caving in to demands for independence on the part of the Tibetan government-in-exile would set a precedent for Xinjiang, another autonomous region with a largely Muslim, ethnically Uyghur population, representing similar problems for Beijing. Linda was tired of hearing the same old conversations over dinner with friends. "It was a standard topic of conversation, somebody would mention that the whole world was against China, and the easiest thing was to go along. We Chinese all get the same education. I would have followed the herd too if I had worked in something else."

Her first month at the station gave her just a taste of what was to come. In 2008, more things happened in China than happen in other countries over the course of a decade. In anticipation of the Olympic Games, many media outlets that had never taken much of an interest in China beyond covering the occasional natural disaster involving thousands of deaths, now began seeking out information on its economic growth, social problems, and that mysterious institution called the Communist Party.

Linda had never seen her own country through the lens of a western television camera. As a production assistant, her job was to look for stories and interview subjects that could be of interest, do research and fact-check, secure permissions to film, and translate the interviews. One of her first assignments was to investigate the forced evictions and land expropriation. Since 2000, tens and perhaps hundreds of thousands of people[8] have been forced from their homes to make way for construction of the Olympic stadiums and to modernize the city. The authorities offered to relocate people in other homes; some accepted, while others didn't. Some families were thrilled to move to a new apartment on the city's outskirts, because at last, they would have a toilet and heat. Others acknowledged that the apartments were nicer, but then they found out it took them an hour longer to get to work, their new surroundings felt strange, and they lost touch with their neighbors. They felt depressed.

Many refused to move because the amount of money they were offered in compensation was absurdly low, not anywhere close to the commercial value of the property. And in some cases, people never saw a single yuan. Linda and her colleagues interviewed people who had resisted, and had been beaten by thugs hired by real estate developers. Some of their neighbors' homes had been bulldozed in the middle of the night. Linda talked with some petitioners who tried to get justice for their cause, much to the authorities' chagrin.[9] "They were just regular people!" she said. "I was struck by how easy it would be to end up like them, losing everything, defenseless." In some neighborhoods with one- or two-story houses still standing in central Beijing, you can still find leaflets with government propaganda: "Take advantage of this opportunity. The sooner you move, the sooner your dreams will come true." "Don't listen to the rumors, trust the Government."

Forced evictions are nothing new in China. Ever since the economic reforms of the 1980s began, at least forty million rural peasants have been forced off of their land.[10] The real estate boom took off in those years. The sector grew and grew, because of two factors: China needed to house more people in its cities, and local governments needed financing. Almost 80% of the urban planning budget was funded by selling land to real estate developers.[11] Local authorities use part of that money to pay fees to the displaced people, and keep the rest. The lower the fees they can get away with, the more cash fills the municipal governments' coffers and the real estate developers' pockets.

In theory, citizens who are not satisfied with the arrangement can file a complaint with the State. In practice, the courts refuse to hear their cases because of pressure from government authorities and business interests. Whoever dares to protest pays a very high price. The government acknowledges that the problem affects the whole country, but they have only instituted minimal legislative reforms. During the Olympic Games, the authorities mandated that the people had the right to demonstrate, as long as they sought permission, and conducted demonstrations in approved areas. But no one was allowed to demonstrate, and the authorities retaliated against anyone who tried. Some citizens were thrown in jail or placed under house arrest for organizing protests, according to Human Rights Watch.

"It's ironic that they say we're living in the 'new China'. Many of our problems, like forced evictions or the inequality between the rich and the poor go back for centuries," Linda observed. Those issues had not directly impacted her. But she would never forget the devastated faces of those who had been beaten down, the grandparents weeping among the ruins that had once been their homes. Most Chinese who work for foreign media companies have had similar experiences. Linda told me they talked about it when they got together for dinner, and on an Internet forum where they gave each other advice and assistance. The year of the Olympics had been especially hard on them. They felt an obligation to cast a spotlight on the atrocities being committed behind the scenes, while also feeling very guilty for criticizing their country, because they believed there were many good things about China, too.

Linda had earned a reputation as being an essential member of the production team where she worked. Many other Western media companies would have snapped her up to be a producer for them: she was fast on her feet, knew how to get to the heart of a story, and when she wanted something, she didn't stop until she got it. But she confessed that she didn't have a vocation for journalism. She hadn't read newspapers as a teenager, and she wasn't one of those curious students who passed banned films and books around among themselves. She only went to work for a foreign media company because she wanted to find out how the world worked.

We had run into each other a few times because of our work, but we had never really talked. At press conferences she sat in the front row, taking notes at a furious pace in her notebook, while answering two phones at the same time. When I first called her, she was very interested in this book project, but she said she did not want to be included in it, for fear that something could happen to her family as a result. Her mother had worked for the government in Wuhan, her native province, and her father had worked for a state-owned company, now they were both retired. But what about her cousins and aunts and uncles? "In China, you never know what the consequences will be for something like this," she told me. Since Linda's story was too good not to include here, I asked her to set the ground rules that would make her feel comfortable enough to participate. There were three: her real name would not be used, the media companies she had worked for would not be specified, and the most dramatic experiences she had had with the authorities would not be mentioned at all.

At our first meeting, we went to a café she liked near the Drum Tower. It was brightly lit, and had a bohemian feel, with mismatched sofas and bookcases. Linda ordered a pear tart and a soft drink, and began asking me questions. It felt like I was the one being interviewed. She wanted to know what I had done before arriving in China, if I had brothers and sisters, how I edited the recording from my digital recorder. She was endlessly curious, very spontaneous and had a great sense of humor. She opened her eyes wide when she talked, and gestured animatedly with her hands. She didn't at all resemble the serious journalist I had seen at the press conferences.

She ate very slowly, methodically picking away at the tart's pastry with her fork, saving the pear filling for last. She told me that ever since she was a little girl, she made decisions with one goal in mind: to learn. No matter what, she had wanted to attend Beida, the University of Beijing, because it seemed to epitomize intellectualism. She got in by applying to one of the most exotic academic departments on the planet: Urdu philology. "Urdu is the unifying language of Pakistan, like Mandarin here in China. It's a mix of Persian and Arabic," she explained. "I already knew Chinese and English, so I looked at the world map and said to myself, I'm going to learn something halfway in between." The University provided her with something she had been long awaiting. "For the first time I had to really think and draw my own conclusions, because up until then, I had just learned everything by rote. It was wonderful to feel that my brain was really alive, questioning everything, as my classmates and professors were doing the same thing. We spent hours reflecting on why people get angry, what exactly is a city, the concept of motherhood. . . . When you start working, you don't have much time for thinking about things that are not immediately useful. My mother wanted me to major in Economics. Maybe it was selfish of me not to have chosen a field that would have allowed me to earn more money and help my family, but I didn't want to end up being a rich person who didn't know anything about the world."

At the time, she hadn't considered journalism as a career option. "I didn't really have a clear understanding of the media, Chinese or foreign. I didn't feel that urge to bring new stories out into the light. I wanted to see the world, have life experiences, and learn." Until something happened that changed her life: Pervez Musharraf, the president of Pakistan at the time, visited Beijing and held a reception for diplomats and foreign policy students. They sent Linda and her classmates an invitation as a courtesy, in the interest of promoting the Urdu language. The event followed the standard protocol, but Musharraf wanted to appear to have an open dialogue, and opened up a round of questions for the students in attendance. Linda raised her hand. "My question was very basic: Mr. President, what do you think the United Nations could do to help solve the problem of terrorism in Pakistan? But I asked in Urdu, and all the diplomats turned to look at me. The room went quiet, and Musharraf answered: Miss, since you speak Urdu much better than I do, allow me to answer in English," she remembered, laughing.

She liked how it felt to question someone she would normally never be able to talk to. "It occurred to me that if I was a reporter, I could get access to people and places." A few months later, at a reception commemorating Pakistan's Independence day, she went up to the Pakistani ambassador in Beijing, and asked if he remembered her. How could I forget the student who had surprised the president, he replied. "I told him when I graduated I wanted to be a journalist, and I asked if he could help me get an internship in Pakistani media."

A few months later she landed in Islamabad.

She arrived on a flight from New Delhi. A Pakistani official was there to meet her at the airport. "He called me by my name in Urdu, Yahaara, which means 'adornment of the Universe.' He picked up my dusty suitcase and we got into a government car. It was the first time I had ever been in a car with a little table in the backseat. On the way to the city, he told me about his country's geography and history, as if I were a diplomat," she recalled. "China and Pakistan have a very special relationship that they want to strengthen in order to put pressure on India. I guess my trip symbolized an act of friendship."

Her escort took her to one of the best hotels in the city. Used to traveling among backpackers, Linda explained that she couldn't stay there. But he told her not to worry, the Ministry of Foreign Affairs was taking care of everything. "It was really funny. I had brought a leftover piece of pizza along with me from New Delhi so I'd have something to eat. This very kind gentleman who had picked me up carried all my luggage in and stood there looking at me in the middle of this very luxurious hotel room, with its king-size bed and sofas. He pointed to the box of pizza and said, "Miss, do you really need that? I think it must be rather cold by now," she giggled at the memory.

Her internship consisted of shadowing the editors of a local newspaper and television news program for a month in Islama-bad, Lahore and Karachi. She would not publish or produce any stories herself, her job was simply to ask questions and take notes. Because of frequent terrorist attacks, she noticed her su-pervisors were very concerned about her security. "They were obsessed about foreigners' safety. In Karachi, my hotel was right in front of the restaurant where they had kidnapped Daniel Pearl, the reporter from *The Wall Street Journal*,"[12] she told me. I asked her if she had been afraid. "I was young and careless. I never thought anything could happen to me. There was an armed soldier with a bayonet stationed right outside of my hotel room. The first day I was there, he knocked on my door and said in Urdu, 'I'm here to protect you. If you go out, I'm going to fol-low you.' I told him I didn't want him to follow me because it would just attract more attention. He said I would have to sign a paper if I didn't want to be guarded. And I signed it. I wouldn't have done that now."

The month spent in Pakistan whetted her appetite for interna-tional journalism. Once back in China, she started researching prestigious journalism schools where she could study. She wasn't accepted at Columbia University, but she did get into a Master's degree program in London, where for the first time she found herself surrounded by news junkies. Her classmates were on top of everything going on all around the world; they recommended hundreds of books and documentary films to her that would change her life. With her heart in her throat, she watched along with her classmates footage from the earthquake in Kashmir that killed more than 75,000 people on October 8, 2005. It was a Saturday, and school was in session in that region between India and Pakistan. The tremors struck while thousands of children were in their classrooms. Reconstruction would be protracted and complicated. Linda spent the following months getting in touch with local reporters she had met during her internship, and making contacts in the Pakistani community in London. She decided her final project for her degree would be producing a documentary on survivors of the earthquake. A few NGOs helped her with the logistics.

"I arrived in the mountains in Kashmir in an old pick-up truck, with a group of people that a humanitarian aid organization had introduced me to," she recalled. "The roads were a disaster. In some sections, you couldn't even see where the edge of the road was. Looking back on it, I don't know how I did it. I traveled around for a month with a camera, tripod, reflectors, and my backpack. I had just learned how to use the camera in a class, and I had never produced a single story. But I dove right in. It was fascinating to be there. I went into refugee camps where the people had lost everything, but they still offered me something to eat from the little they had. The whole time I kept thinking, I'm so lucky to be here seeing this. There are so many different lives in this world."

She submitted her film to Al Jazeera's New Horizon International Documentary Film Festival. The Al Jazeera network wasn't as well known internationally then as it is now, but it had a good reputation among her classmates in London. "They said it was cutting-edge, and impartial compared to the BBC and CNN," Linda explained. She wanted to stay in London and get a job, but it was hard for a Chinese citizen to get a visa. "My student visa was going to expire in a few months, and they told me my film had been nominated to be screened at the festival, which was in Doha. If I left the United Kingdom, they wouldn't let me back in. But something told me I had to go, so I packed all my things, stored the boxes in my boyfriend at the time's room, and went to the festival."

One thing led to another. At the festival she met her future boss, who was very impressed with the bright girl who spoke perfect Mandarin, Urdu and English. Al Jazeera's office in Beijing had a job opening for an assistant, and she seemed like the perfect candidate. For Linda, it was the ideal opportunity to get into international journalism without taking too many risks. Al Jazeera had been launched with the mission of countering the dominant Anglo-Saxon voice in international news, and at that time the company had a relatively untroubled relationship with the Chinese government.[13] In the eight months she worked in the Beijing office, Linda hardly ever left the editing room. Her job was to do research for stories and translate. "It was interesting, but I wanted more. At twenty years old, once you have learned how to do something, you need to advance to the next level. A position opened up at an American network, and I applied for it."

Her life would have been very different if she worked for the local Chinese media, mainly because a Chinese reporter's first mission is not to present the facts objectively, but to "serve socialism and the Communist Party," as President Hu Jintao himself put it shortly before the 2008 Olympic Games. In journalism school, students are required to sit through many hours of ideological education. A young aspiring reporter in Beijing once told me that no one in her class wanted to cover politics, because the pressure was unbearable. She had specialized in sports, while her friends had focused on entertainment and economics. Financial reporting also seemed like a good option: journalism students unabashedly recognized that companies tried to buy reporters with lavish gifts and trips.

A Chinese reporter cannot directly embarrass a politician. Beijing expects reporters to act as the government's right arm, helping them to influence public opinion. Anything beyond that is taking a risk. When it comes to freedom of the press, China is in poor company: the country ranks 174 out of 179 on the list compiled by Reporters Without Borders, ahead of only Iran, Syria, Turkmenistan, North Korea and Eritrea.[14] At least twenty-six reporters are currently in prison for writing articles on democracy, the Tiananmen Square massacre, environmental scandals, ethnic uprisings or stories that implicated the Communist Party.[15] A dramatic example was the case of writer Tan Zuoren, famous among activists, who traveled to Sichuan after the May 2008 earthquake. Over 5,000 children died, buried in rubble after the collapse of their schools, which had been built with cheap, poor-quality materials and shoddily constructed because of local corruption. Tan wrote a report chronicling the scandal, and the Government moved to silence him. He was sentenced to a five-year prison term in 2010.[16]

Every day, Chinese media companies receive direct instructions from the Department of Propaganda on what news stories they can cover, and how, in communications like this:

"All media should report on land expropriations very carefully. Do not question legitimate demolitions, do not support those who demand unreasonable compensation, do not report on incidents related to forced demolitions, such as suicides, self-inflicted injuries by the residents or protests. Do not highlight the few extreme cases. Stories on the subject or drawing connections between isolated incidents will not be tolerated."

Or:

"Regarding the fatal incident on the Ministry of Railways' train K256 from Shanghai in which a passenger died after an altercation with crew members, the media will not conduct independent investigations, but will wait for the Ministry's press release."[17]

Journalists and Web surfers sarcastically refer to the Department of Propaganda as *zhenli bu* (真理部), the Ministry of Truth, a nod to George Orwell's classic novel *1984*. One anonymous blogger maintains a blog called Zhenli Bu, which posts all the subjects of potential news stories forbidden by the Department of Propaganda.[18] It is one of the best tools for discovering what really goes on inside Chinese media.

Taiwan, Xinjiang and Tibet top the list of most delicate subjects for Chinese reporters. The island of Taiwan has been in practice an independent state since the fifties, but China considers it a rebel province. Beijing has claimed Taiwan as its own since the civil war ended in 1949, when the defeated nationalists took refuge on the island as Mao Zedong rose to power on continental China. Since 2009, relations between Taipei and Beijing have greatly improved, with direct flights between both cities, and a free trade agreement in place, albeit with many restrictions. But the battle lines are still drawn: China has hundreds of missiles aimed at Taiwan, and declares it will take the territory back by force if necessary. The United States is Taiwan's closest ally, and its main arms supplier.

Xinjiang poses a problem similar to Tibet for the Communist Party. Both are autonomous regions, occupying strategic locations on the map, with substantial reserves of natural gas and petroleum. Xinjiang enjoyed some periods of independence over the course of its long history, but it was overtaken by the Chinese in

the eighteenth century. Since the 1950s, Beijing has actively encouraged the migration of ethnic Han to the region, where Muslim Uyghurs are the ethnic majority. They speak Uyghur, a
Turkic language, and are deeply nationalist. Heading their advo-
cacy organization in exile, the World Uyghur Congress, is Rebiya
Kadeer, known as the "Mother of the Uyghur Diaspora". In 2009
ethnic violence broke out, and dozens of Uyghurs and Han Chinese have been killed, hundreds have been arrested, and the province was locked down and shut off from the rest of the country for
months.

All information on these three subjects is absolutely controlled
by the government. But there are more. For example, in cases of
accidents or disasters, all media outlets have to wait for the Government's official statement on the matter, or go by what is broadcast on the official Xinhua agency or CCTV channel. Making
direct contact with journalists in the affected area is not allowed.
News items on forced evictions, or on environmental degradation
or contamination of foods have to always follow the official party
rhetoric, and "not mention any extreme cases." At least a hundred
thousand massive protests are staged every year according to the
Academy of Social Sciences, but the media must not interpret
them collectively as a social problem.[19] Reporters are forbidden
from employing the term "civil society," they cannot question political reforms or adopt a posture contrary to the Government's
position. Editors who do not obey these rules are fired. Some col-
umnists in the past have been ostracized for refusing to tone down
their opinions.

It's a depressing state of affairs, many journalists acknowledge.
Most reporters eventually resign themselves to writing what they
are told to write, and supplement their salaries by attending all the
press conferences they can, where companies pass out the ubiqui-
tous red envelopes stuffed with cash. The bribes are so common-

place that reporters feel no embarrassment at all in accepting them. A friend of Linda's who worked at the British daily *The Financial Times* had a surreal experience at a press conference in Beijing. The company which had organized the press conference handed her a dossier filled with business information, and a red envelope. She went back to the desk manned by public relations staffers to return it. They insisted that she keep it. As they were going back and forth, she overheard two other local reporters arguing with another woman behind the PR desk. "It's not fair," they said, "we're from the same newspaper but we work in different sections, so how come we just got a single red envelope?"

Between the journalists who become ardent activists and sacrifice their jobs and the ones who keep their heads down and do as they are told, lies a group in the middle: the reporters who get some measure of satisfaction from scoring a point against the forces of censorship every once in a while. In 1991, several editorials published in *People's Daily*, the voice of the Communist Party, under the name Huangfu Ping caused an uproar, as they praised Deng Xiaoping's controversial initiatives to open the economy. The author of the articles was actually Zhou Ruijin, the paper's former editor-in-chief, who did not dare sign his real name, but succeeded in stirring up heated debate within and outside the Party for months. In June 2011 *Guiji Xianqu Daobao* columnist Xiao De wrote that Chinese society was becoming "unlivable." And as far as the dismal state of some local governments, he asserted, "When a State official's sole objective is to accept bribes, we should not be at all surprised that he governs in a ridiculous manner, with no conscience or scruples, not acting as a guardian of the law. Passing laws is easy; building a common moral foundation is much harder."

The boundaries are not always clearly marked, but everyone knows some subjects are inherently risky. In 2010, the magazine

Caijing published a special feature[20] on corruption in government over the last twenty years, but it never questions the legitimacy of the Communist Party. The Internet, censured but with more gray areas, is allowed to venture farther. Chinese people have been able to read wonderful investigative reports, thanks to the micro blogs. It can take the censors a few hours to block a Web page containing information perceived as damaging to the government, and journalists take advantage of this small window to get information out there. Thanks to the Internet, editors like Zhang Hong, Assistant Director of the weekly *The Economic Observer*, discreetly gets stories out there that he believes the people need to know about. When the nuclear disaster in Fukushima, Japan happened in March, 2011, sales of salt skyrocketed in some Chinese cities because people believed ingesting iodine could reduce the possibility of contracting radiation sickness. *The Economic Observer* published a report titled, "Panic in Canton, Shenzhen and Dongguan; Iodized Salt Runs Out; Nuclear Panic in Japan Grows." Within a matter of minutes, Zhang Hong got a call from the censors. The government did not want to alarm the public. So Zhang Hong changed part of the headline, so it read: "Panic in Canton, Shenzhen and Dongguan; Authorities Say Salt Supplies are Sufficient," but he did not change the body of the article at all. Reporters know these are small victories, but insist they have to start somewhere.

"When some foreigners criticize Chinese journalists, and lump us all into the same category, I feel really bad. There are some really fine investigative reporters in this country, and they risk their lives. It's very easy to criticize Chinese journalism from a distance," Linda said. In her opinion, you couldn't blame people for not wanting to get into any trouble. "I think that as journalists we need to push the envelope as far as we can, and challenge power. But we shouldn't expect everybody to want to do this. I think foreigners should stop trying to lecture us on journalism, because you don't get anything for free here."

Foreign correspondents are treated far better than local Chinese reporters. But that doesn't mean it's easy to work there. Because of censorship, Internet service is frequently interrupted, especially as important symbolic dates approach, like the anniversary of the Tiananmen Square massacre. The bureaucracy is maddening, and access to government officials is extremely limited. Landing an interview with a Ministry head would be unthinkable. At the most, an interview with one of his underlings might be granted, and in that case all the questions and a proposal detailing the purpose of the interview would have to be faxed in advance to several staffers to ensure that no one along the chain of command is offended. Dealing with academics could not be more different, as they are almost always happy to talk.

Many foreign media companies have their bureaus in ancient diplomatic compounds. A French reporter once found an old, rusting microphone behind the air conditioner in his office. It must have been put back there years ago to spy on some foreign official, but for a while we joked that we had to stay on our toes, because Big Brother was always watching us. All joking aside, it is a fact that some foreign reporters' emails and phone lines are monitored. Chinese authorities sometimes call Chinese assistants working for foreign media companies to drag information out of them: what is that foreign reporter working on, who is she talking to, when will the article be published. They are often offered money in exchange for details.

It is very hard for a foreigner to go unnoticed. Especially outside of the major cities, a foreigner wandering around certain areas attracts a great deal of attention. From the moment a foreigner registers in a hotel with his passport, the hotel staff has to let the local police know that they have a journalist staying there. Within a matter of hours the reporter finds himself on a plane or train, being sent back to where he came from. It is fairly routine for foreign journalists to hear a knock on their hotel door in the middle of the night, as the police hustle them out of town before they get the chance to cover a sensitive story.

Beijing has pledged to ensure the security of foreign journalists, and to an extent they do manage it, at least in the major cities. But rural areas are no-man's land. In February 2012, a Dutch reporter, a French reporter and his Chinese assistant were all assaulted in the same week while they covered some forced land expropriations in Panhe, in Zhejiang province. The French reporter said that around twenty or thirty men attacked him, and he believed they were policemen out of uniform and hired thugs. They ripped the camera out of his assistant's hands and struck him on the head with it until blood dripped down his face. They confiscated their notebooks and memory cards. They beat up the Dutch reporter too, and took the documents the dispossessed peasants had given him to prove their cases. The police broke up the melee, but the reporters never got their memory cards back with the footage they had shot. They gave the French reporter 45,000 yuan ($7,150) for the broken camera. The police officers insisted that it was the townspeople themselves who had been the aggressors.

For any journalists working in China, their biggest worry is putting their sources in danger. If just before a scheduled interview, the interviewee stops answering the phone and disappears, it's almost always because they have received threats. The worst-case scenario happened to a peasant called Fu Xiancai. Like millions of rural poor, Fu was forced off his land to make way for the Three Gorges Dam. In 2005, he told an American reporter that the government had given him a shamefully low payoff, and relocated him next to a contaminated river. There were many cases of liver cancer among his new neighbors. After the interview, Fu Xiancai found himself in the crosshairs of the local authorities, who threatened him for months. One day he came home to find a pile of spirit money on his doorstep, a symbolic threat, because these false bills are burned at funerals in China. He was attacked by thugs, and fractured a leg. But he did not give in, and the following year Fu Xiancai talked to the German network ARD. Shortly after that, he was beaten so savagely he was left a quadriplegic. The case had diplomatic repercussions. According to the German network Deutsche Welle, Berlin demanded an explanation from Beijing through their embassy. And Germany covered part of the cost of Fu Xiancai's surgery, although he would never walk again. The official report from the Chinese government stated that he had caused his own injuries.

Chinese assistants working for foreign media companies are in a very tough position. They are not offered any additional security for working with foreigners. Some quit, overwhelmed by the fear and stress the job entails. An acquaintance of mine left her job translating for a foreign television network because a government ministry suggested that her brother, who was going to take the civil service exam, "might not pass after all." When Linda started out at a job as a production assistant, she had an experience that deeply affected her. It was the twenty-year anniversary of the Tiananmen Square massacre, and she wanted to go see the demonstration that mothers of the victims always held every year outside the Muxidi metro stop, where in 1989 troops fired on protesters.

"I wasn't going for work, I just wanted to see it for myself," she told me. "From a distance I saw some foreigners I knew, and I waved to them. Just then, a police officer rushed up to me and asked to see my papers. I told him I was on my way home and just happened to be passing by. He asked me how I knew those people.

He wanted to know where I worked. He didn't believe me, he was very agitated. Finally another officer came over, he looked like a decent sort and he told me to go home right away. Maybe they take different roles; good cop, bad cop. The one that seemed to be in charge said to me, if you don't go now, you'll suffer the consequences. A lot of things could happen to you."

Ever since then, Linda takes certain precautions when she works. She doesn't surf the Internet at home, and she doesn't accompany all the interview subjects to their interviews with reporters. "When I was younger, I thought nothing would happen to me as long as I didn't do anything wrong. Now I think there are consequences and collateral damage for everything. I am Chinese, and I can't go to certain places, and for others it's best if I go along with a foreigner. I shouldn't try to be first in line for anything, because I'd have to pay a much higher price. A foreign correspondent could be blacklisted, and expelled from the country. But I'm here, and my family is here. An assistant who worked for *The New York Times* spent three years in jail. They accused him of leaking information. That gives you some idea of what the government can do to us."

Linda's view of China has changed over the four years she has been working for foreign media. "I'd like to say it has been enhanced. Before, there were a lot of little things that I didn't notice at all," she gestured to my digital recorder, to make sure I didn't forget to register that. We were talking over mojitos in Nanluoguxiang, a street filled with stylish bars, trying to escape the early summer heat. A Bob Marley song played over the sound system as the waiter, his hair tied back in a ponytail, sifted through a stack of vinyl records. Linda asked for some more ice for her drink. She had spent the morning at an outdoor wedding, and was still feeling the heat. She dabbed at her forehead with a perfectly ironed floral handkerchief, and took a handful of candies out of her bag. "Try them, they gave them out at the wedding. They're really good, but they stick to your teeth," she giggled, and pretended to chew like a camel.

She could say she had realized the dream she had had as a student, putting the pieces of the puzzle together and having a better understanding of the world around her. "Now I know more about my country, and I understand why people act the way they do. In restaurants, waiters are usually really grumpy. Some are just rude, but many are migrants from the countryside and they have a million problems, discrimination, loneliness, no social benefits, low wages. And all of that puts them in a bad mood."

Linda had interviewed multimillionaires, and people who had lost everything. Her job gave her access to clandestine places and incriminating documents. It was a more intense lifestyle than many of her friends had. But it came at a price: it meant questioning everything, every day.

"I remember during the Olympic Games we filmed a group of volunteers singing. There were elderly people, adults and children. Everyone was so excited to be on television, and they really hoped foreign countries would start talking about China. I knew we would include the footage in a report criticizing many of the government's mistakes, which were undeniable: expulsions, corruption, censorship. I had mixed feelings because in any case, in that moment, those volunteers were happy. No doubt they didn't realize they were the Party's pawns, just puppets on strings. Something similar happened with the construction workers who built the stadiums. They were happy to do their jobs, and make some money, period. They didn't think about the workplace exploitation that the West was talking about. It's hard to explain all of those nuances in a two-minute segment."

Linda was deeply affected by the case of Liu Xiaobo, winner of the Nobel Peace Prize in 2010, who was serving a prison sentence for his writings advocating for democracy and the end of the one-party system. When the prize was announced, she was one of the few Chinese journalists who went to his wife's house in Beijing. She was under house arrest, and could not go outside to talk to them. The police blocked off the street, so no one could access it. "We were all there, waiting. When the Nobel committee made the announcement, I felt conflicted. As a Chinese person, it was a huge deal and so wonderful that they were giving the prize to someone from my country. At the same time it was pathetic to see all those police guarding their building. Some of them were really young, and might not have had any idea about what was actually going on. They had just gotten orders to not let any of those crazy foreigners on the block. They were just doing their job, it wasn't their fault. It was everyone's fault, for letting the system be what it is."

Her bosses had warned her that the job entailed taking certain risks. But no one had explained that she would have to deal with the ire of her fellow countrymen. When her friends criticized foreign journalists, she had to bite her tongue. "Some networks make mistakes, but the people I have worked with are honorable. If they don't cover a story in enough depth, it's because of limitations imposed by the network, requiring short news segments, not because they're not impartial." Inevitably, she has distanced herself from certain people. Some of her old classmates ended up going to work for the State Security Department and the Ministry of Foreign Affairs.

Two twenty-something guys leaned against a car smoking just outside the Mao Live House, one of the best live music venues in Beijing. One had his hair styled in a Mohawk dyed bright fuchsia, and wore a studded jacket and spandex pants that clung to his spindly legs. His friend wore sunglasses even though it was almost dark. In the summer, Gulou Street is a colorful spectacle at that hour. As I waited for Linda, dozens of scenes unfolded before my eyes. Local residents without air conditioning had brought little stools to sit on out onto the sidewalk. Some elderly men with their shirts tied above their waists fanned themselves with folding fans. Techno music blared from a hair salon, distorted and metallic. The speakers were outside to attract customers, but they weren't very good and couldn't handle the high volume. A couple wearing matching pajamas and rubber slippers ambled by, walking their dog. A delivery man on a motorized bike ran a red light and very narrowly missed getting hit by a bus, which also didn't stop. Then Linda appeared at the end of the block.

She was dressed in a green blouse and loose-fitting pants. It was her day off, and she had been doing yoga and reading Edward Said. "I find his book *Orientalism* absolutely fascinating. Do you know it? He talks about the romantic image of Asia and the prejudices Westerners had about the Middle East, that they used to justify colonialism. It's really interesting."

Conversations with Linda could go off in a hundred directions. She would start with one idea, and that led to another. When she paused, it seemed as if she was getting ready to launch into whole new territory. "I don't know if this happens you," she remarked as we walked, "but doing journalism, you realize that you're not creating. You observe, and transmit, but you stay on the margins so you can be objective, and you're not building anything. I wonder if this is what I want to do for the rest of my life."

"Are you thinking about quitting your job?" I asked, puzzled. She had a position that many people would give their right arms for.

She laughed.

"It's just a thought, don't worry. But yes, I have thought about it a lot. When things with the government get tense, I think it's not worth it. I've seen so many things in the last few years that have really made a mark on me. Activists that have fought for a long time become hardened. I don't want to be a bitter person. I don't want to be that type of woman. I want to keep on marveling over things. We only have one life to live."

Acknowledgments

This book would not exist if the ten people whose stories fill these pages had not been willing to talk to me. Several of them took serious risks to meet with me, and even so they were extremely generous with their time, offering as many details as they could. When I couldn't understand a particular word, they made an effort to express themselves in simpler language. I might not talk to some of them ever again, because they don't have email, or because they often change their phone numbers. And I hope to never see some of their names in the press, because that would mean they have been detained. I want to thank all of them for their wholehearted commitment.

I'd like to thank two people who were instrumental in this book's preparation: a young man, Jia Wen and a young woman, Liu Chengxi, both from humble backgrounds who made considerable sacrifices to have the opportunity to work in Beijing. They helped translate some interviews, and explained a great deal about the Chinese people and their culture. They were both fascinated by the fact that I was working on a book about the *laobaixing*, common, everyday people.

Wu Rong Rong, the sociologist in Chapter Eight, traveled over a thousand miles to accompany me to places I never could have entered on my own. It was the first time she had been apart from her three-month-old son, and I know that was very hard on her, but she thought it was very important to show me what the lives of Chinese prostitutes were really like. To legal expert Lan Yujiao, who patiently explained the many forms repression of pro–human rights lawyers could take. My dear friend Xiao Ma introduced me to his kung-fu master, featured in Chapter Four. Xiao Ma exemplifies how deeply loyal the Chinese are once they offer their friendship. I will always remember his wonderful sense of humor and sincerity.

Thanks to the writer Mariela Dabbah, for her spirit and generosity. To Erik Riesenberg and Carlos Azula of C. A. Press at Penguin Group (USA), and my agent, Diane Stockwell, because they saw these ten stories needed to be told as clearly as I did. To my editor, Adriana V. Lopez, who rigorously and adeptly dissected the text.

I could not have written this book without my fellow journalists of the "Beijinderberg Club" either. We worked on grueling assignments, had passionate debates, and, most of all, laughed late into the night together. Miguel Torán was a solid support during the hardest weeks of research. Ángel Villarino, Aritz Parra, Alberto Lebrón and Juan Pablo Cardenal shared their knowledge of China and were instrumental to me, along with Cristina Martí. Iris Mir and Olatz Simon knew just how to encourage me from afar. Virginia Casado and David Brunat opened their home to me and infused me with energy. I admire them all, and am grateful for their friendship.

Thanks to Gregorio Doval, Ana Pérez, Silvia Blanco, María Carmona and Darío Ochoa for their patience and input, and for being so generous with their time. To Daniel Méndez, creator of Zai China, who shared his thoughts on Chinese Internet users.

To my brother, Andrés, for showing such genuine enthusiasm from the beginning of the project, and for helping me translate the martial arts terms in Chapter Four. To Sabela, who moved heaven and earth to help. To Berta, for wanting to follow along the whole process. To my parents, for understanding why I was going so far away, and for having faith in me.

To Mario Saavedra, the smartest person I know, who, luckily, shares his life with me. For listening, reading, rereading, taking me outside to get some sun when my face started to look green, and for doing all the things that make him the best thing that's ever happened to me.

Notes

1. Rich Kids

1. Those cities are located in the center, south, and northeast of China, respectively.
2. According to a feature in *Hurun*, of the 1,330 Chinese millionaires or multimillionaires classified as such by the magazine between 1999 and 2008, thirty-six later found themselves in trouble with the law. In August 2009, sixteen of them were in prison; three were awaiting sentencing, and ten were under official investigation. Seven had disappeared or had left the country because they had charges pending.
3. In 2011, almost 2,700 millionaires from mainland China applied for an investor visa. One thousand of them were granted one.
4. The demand has exploded at such a rate that some countries put strict limits on the numbers of foreign investor visas. In July 2011, Canada announced it would grant only seven hundred such visas. Within one week of the announcement, they had reached their quota: 697 applications had come from China.
5. Until 2008, land use was conceded for a maximum of seventy years. In January 2008, the new private property law stipulated that the concession would be automatically renewed when the end of the period was reached, assuaging insecurity among residents. In practice, land concession now more closely resembles actual private property ownership, although it doesn't quite get there.

6. Jianzhen brought Buddhism to China in the eighth century.
7. The island of Hainan is one of the most popular honeymoon destinations among the Chinese.

2. Kidnapped by His Own Government

1. Of the roughly 200,000 lawyers in China, only two hundred are a part of the civil rights movement, or *wéiquán* (维权). They must deal with police harassment, and are in constant danger of being kidnapped, tortured, or placed under house arrest.

2. The Web site Boxun, run by exiled dissidents and censured in China, called for citizens to stage protests in thirteen cities across the country. But there were only signs of protest in Beijing and Shanghai, on commercial streets, so it was hard to tell how many people were protesting, and how many were just shopping. In Beijing, police and special agents swarmed over Wangfujing Avenue. Several passersby and journalists were taken into custody. The police and officials from the Ministry of Security interrogated and threatened many foreign journalists for covering the story.

3. In theory, the law prohibits the use of force or coercion against women to make them get an abortion or undergo sterilization. But the pressure to comply with the one-child policy was so great that it was brutally enforced by local authorities in some areas of China. If a family already had two children, for example, one of the parents would be forced to undergo sterilization.

4. Chen somehow managed to get by the guards posted at his front door. Supported and aided by a network of activists, he reached Beijing and was granted asylum at the U.S. Embassy. His case raised tensions between China and the United States, which negotiated allowing Chen to leave the country, traveling to New York.

5. The Chinese security and counterespionage apparatus is comprised of the Ministry of Public Security, the Ministry of State Security, and the Police. The Ministry of State Security is a department of the State Council and its responsibilities include monitoring dissidents, foreign journalists, and civil rights lawyers. Its budget is larger than any other Ministry.

6. Richardson, Sophie, ed. *An Alleyway in Hell: China's Abusive "Black Jails."* New York: Human Rights Watch, 2009.

7. China's national flag.

8. Falun Gong (法轮功) or Falun Dafa (法轮大法) is a Buddhist-inspired spiritual movement. Beijing considers it a "diabolical cult" and has banned its practice since 1999. Some experts believe the Communist Party is worried that the movement, that has anywhere between three and seventy million followers, could challenge its authority. According to various human rights organizations and the U.S. State Department, hundreds or perhaps thousands of Falun Gong sympathizers have died while in police custody.

9. Mao wanted to regain power, which he had lost after the failure of his Great Leap Forward. In 1966, he urged the army and young students (known as the Red Guards) to shun everything that strayed from the true spirit of the revolution. He was supported by the Gang of Four, a group of Party leaders which included his wife.

10. The Great Leap Forward was a series of economic, social, and political measures enacted by Mao Zedong in the late fifties and early sixties. The goal was to make full use of China's enormous human capital in the service of industrialization. Mao assured that China would be on the level of Great Britain within fifteen years. The program's failure, coupled with a series of natural disasters and China's break with the Soviet Union, caused a famine which killed between twenty and thirty million people.

11. The film was outlawed after the Tiananmen Square massacre and is still banned to this day. The filmmakers were imprisoned or left the country.

12. At that time, most foreign journalists spoke Mandarin and many were of Asian descent, so the police often mistakenly believed they were local citizens. Jan Wong, a Canadian correspondent for *The Globe and Mail* from 1988 and 1994, recounted how authorities tried to kidnap her in broad daylight in her book *China: Reports from a Not-So-Foreign Correspondent*, Doubleday Canada, 1999.

13. Thousands of people were taken into custody after Tiananmen. Some are still in jail, and others left the country. The families of the victims have never received an official apology from the Government. Some political leaders, acting on their own, have offered monetary compensation to the Mothers of Tiananmen, in exchange for keeping a low profile.

14. Beginning in 1979, couples in China were only allowed to have one child, unless both partners were only children, peasants, members of an ethnic minority, or if they pay a fine (that is how upper-class families in

the cities get around it). Millions of families do not "declare" more than one child, and enforcement of the law has been lax in many provinces. In some towns, however, atrocities like the ones reported by Chen Guangcheng have been committed.

15. Peasants used the term *guizi* (鬼子),"devil," a incredibly pejorative term to call foreigners, meaning invaders. It's a word charged with racial deprecation and historic symbolism. For example, that is what the Japanese soldiers occupying northeast China from 1931 until 1945 were called.

16. The self-critique or *jiantao* (检讨) was a routine practice during Mao's rule, as in other authoritarian regimes.

3. A Gay Husband Is Better Than None

1. *Tongqi* (同妻) is a term in the popular lexicon which comes from combining *tongzhi* (同志 literally, comrade, but it is also used to refer to a gay man), and *qizi* (妻子, wife).

2. Not his real name.

3. Li Yu Gang is one of the most famous transvestite singers in China. He combines traditional opera with pop music.

4. Owning a home and car is a nonnegotiable requirement for many young Chinese women, and a major source of stress to their suitors. In late 2009, the song "I Don't Have a Car or a House" (没有车没有房), in which the singer Sun Hui lamented about his hardships, became a big hit on the Internet.

5. The Little Red Book is a symbol of Maoism. It was published in 1964, and is a compilation of quotations of then-president Mao Zedong. The Chinese call it *hong baoshu* (红宝书), literally "Precious Red Book." It was required reading in schools for years. Members of the Communist Party were required to always carry it with them.

6. Friends and married couples in China colloquially refer to each other as brother and sister.

7. Mencius was a disciple of Confucius, and lived from 372–289 B.C.

8. During the first three months of 2011, there were 17% more divorces than in the same period in 2010, according to the Ministry of Civil Affairs. Beijing has the highest divorce rate, with 39% of marriages ending in divorce.

4. Silence, the Master Speaks

1. Kung fu (功夫) is the popular term for Chinese martial arts. There are dozens of styles, each with their own organizations and schools.
2. The internal martial arts are *baguazhang* (八卦掌), *taijiquan* (太极拳), *xinyiquan* (形意拳) and *yiquan* (意拳). They focus on channeling the body's internal energy, while the external arts focus on cardiovascular exercise and working the muscles.
3. The Qing dynasty (1644–1912) was the last of the imperial dynasties.
4. To some experts, *mianzhang* (綿掌) or "cotton palm" is a striking technique, not a martial art in itself. There are many different classifications and theories on the martial arts which contradict one another.
5. *Neijiaquan* (內家拳) is an internal martial art.
6. Historically it is not certain that that was the actual origin of *xinyi*. Some theories posit the martial art was created during the Song Dynasty (960–1279 BC).
7. *Wu de* (武 德) is a code of actions as well as thought. A good martial arts student should cultivate morality in both aspects. In his acts, he should exhibit humility, respect, rectitude, trustworthiness, and loyalty. In his thoughts, he should develop a strong will, endurance, perseverance, patience, and bravery.
8. Unless stated otherwise, the doctors referred to in this book are always practitioners of traditional Chinese medicine.
9. From a study published by MIT in February 2012.
10. According to the State news agency Xinhua, authorities have promised to take 1.6 million old vehicles out of circulation, limit the consumption of coal to 10 million tons per year, and plant 328,000 acres of forest, all by 2020.
11. The new measurement standards include particles that are 98 micro inches in diameter or less, also known as PM 2.5. Until January 2012, the Chinese authorities only measured particles larger than 393 micro inches.
12. *Meibanfa* (没办法), loosely translated, "what can you do," "that's life," is a very common Chinese expression.
13. Mrs. Feng always calls her husband "old man" (*lao tou*, 老头) as a term of endearment.
14. "Uncle" and "aunt," a familiar and respectful way the Chinese address their elders.

5. Plunging into the Sea of Business: China's Entrepreneurs

1. *Wanshiruyi* (万事如意) is a very common *chengyu* or idiomatic expression that means "may all your dreams come true." These kinds of expressions are very popular. As a part of China's most cultural elite society, Yang Lu peppers her conversation with even little-known *chengyu*, full of historical references, that most of her compatriots wouldn't understand.

2. Her employees address her as Professor, a term of respect for a teacher, because she gives lectures.

3. The Wheel of Life is a Buddhist diagram consisting of four concentric circles. It symbolizes the cycle of existence, the path to liberation and enlightenment.

4. Based on a survey on worker absenteeism throughout the world conducted by the US consulting firm Kronos.

5. This era and its effects on Chinese society is discussed in more detail in Chapter Nine.

6. The decade of the eighties, up until the Tiananmen Square massacre in 1989, was characterized by its openness (up to a certain limit, because censorship was still in place).

7. In 1980, special economic zones were established in Shenzhen, Zhuhai and Shantong, in the Canton province; Xiamen, in the Fujian province, and on the island of Hainan. They offered land, a cheap labor force, and financial incentives to attract foreign companies. The model was extended to other cities throughout the country.

8. Some foreign companies had maintained business relationships with China since the fifties.

9. In 1998 there were 300,000 Chinese companies owned by the State. In 2008 there were 150,000. (Mark Leonard, *What Does China Think?* HarperCollins, 2008.)

10. *Ibid.*

11. From *The Economist*, citing Zheng Yumin, the ranking Communist Party functionary from Zhejiang, in March, 2011.

12. State-owned companies are on average fourteen times bigger than private companies. (*State-owned Enterprises in China: How Profitable Are They?* by Gao Xu, former economist with the World Bank in Beijing, 2010.)

13. "Entrepreneurship in China." *The Economist*, March, 2011.

14. According to a survey conducted by the China Association of Industry and Commerce, cited by the newspaper *China Daily* (March 14, 2012).

15. According to the investment bank UBS in October, 2011.

16. According to a report produced by the local Wenzhou government and cited by *The New York Times*, ninety business owners fled the city. Several more tried to commit suicide and two of those succeeded.

17. The expression "iron rice bowl" (*tiefanwan*, 铁饭碗) is generally used to describe positions in the Administration or in the Military, which offer employment, a fixed salary and benefits for life. It symbolizes the employment stability and economic privileges of a certain sector of the population, and is the subject of great debate within China.

18. Data from SOHO in February 2012.

19. "Meet Zhang Xin, China's Self-Made Billionairess," by Peter Foster. *The Telegraph*, June 27, 2010.

20. In 2010 one widely commented on story involved the suicide of several workers subcontracted by Apple Foxconn, who allegedly killed themselves because of their horrible work conditions.

21. "The Rise of China's Yuppie Corps: Top CEOs to Watch," by Cheng Li. *China Leadership Monitor*, 2005, No. 14.

22. "While Communist Party regulations call for top officials to disclose their wealth and that of their immediate family members, no law or regulation prohibits relatives of even the most senior officials from becoming deal-makers or major investors—a loophole that effectively allows them to trade on their family name." For the complete article, see "Billions in Hidden Riches for Family of Chinese Leader," by David Barboza, *The New York Times*, October 25, 2012.

23. Statement from a Communist Party spokesperson at the opening of the XVII Congress in 2007.

24. Interview with the Chinese Web site Netease. http://news.163.com /special/lishufu.

25. "What We Really Need To Fear About China," by Vivek Wadhawa. *The Washington Post*, September, 2011.

26. Not her real name.

6. Living Underground

1. In 1978, Deng Xiaoping began to open China's economy. It was the first step in the largest urbanization process in history, and some point to it as the beginning of the country's economic miracle. To many China experts, however, it really began in 1949 with the Maoist revolution. Without that period and the communes of the 1950s, they assert, modernization would not have been possible.

2. Economic reforms picked up speed during the nineties, as many state-run factories shut down, others were consolidated, the agricultural sector was deregulated, and foreign capital began entering China through joint ventures. Unemployment skyrocketed, and millions of uneducated Chinese who until then had held the proverbial "iron rice bowl", a job for life at a state-run factory (see Chapter Five)—were thrown out into the streets. For many, emigration to the cities was the only option.

3. It is customary to give sums of money which contain the numbers 6, 8, or 9 because they are considered lucky (the pronunciation of their characters sounds similar the characters for "fluidity", in a business sense, "prosperity" and "eternity"). The Chinese are very superstitious about numbers. For example, they are often willing to pay much more than the going rate for a license plate or a phone number as long as it includes lucky numbers. On the other hand, buildings generally do not have a fourth floor, they call it 3-B, because the word "four" sounds very similar to the word for "death".

4. In China a red envelope (*hong bao*, 红抱) is used to give cash gifts. These are typically given for weddings, birthdays, and at the New Year.

5. The South-North Water Transfer Project (*Nanshui Beidiao Gongcheng*, 南水北调工程) was a dream of Mao Zedong in 1952, but it was not set in motion until 2002. It is a massive public works project that will send water from the Yangtze River to the northern regions, plagued by recurring droughts. It is controversial because of its high cost, and social and ecological impact. Hundreds of thousands of people have had to abandon their homes, or will have to eventually, since their towns will be submerged under water. It is estimated that in 2050, when the project is complete, 264 gallons of water annually will be diverted to the north.

6. In the country, first-born males are still preferred, because it is believed they can help more with farm work and raising livestock.

7. It was the capital of thirteen dynasties, among them the Zhou, Qin, Han, Sui and Tang.

8. Jackie Chan has a good relationship with the Chinese government, and is the President of the Association of Film Directors. He is known for making provocative statements. In 2009, for example, he said he wasn't entirely sure that freedom was a good thing for China. "I'm starting to think that we Chinese need to be controlled. If we're not controlled, we'll just do whatever we want." He also once stated that he would not buy a Chinese television, because it might explode.

9. On the Gregorian calendar it falls on different dates every year, always between January 21 and February 20, coinciding with the second full moon after the winter solstice.

10. It is known as *chunyun* (春运), the migration for the Spring Festival or the Lunar New Year. Some migrants travel home with thousands of yuan stuffed into their pockets. Robbers know this, and are out in full force traveling the railways at this time of year.

11. In June 2010, a wave of worker strikes swept through foreign factories (Foxconn and Honda, among others) across China. The *mingong* paralyzed production lines, demanding higher wages and better working conditions. Some companies raised salaries as much as 70%. The Chinese government clamped down on the strikes, fearing that the workers would form unions, and could challenge the authority of the Communist Party, but at the same time they raised the minimum wage in many cities to placate migrant workers, a key component of China's economy.

12. The residency permit, called *hukou* (户口), is a kind of internal passport created by Mao Zedong in the fifties, to prevent a mass exodus of people from the countryside heading to the cities when the country was recovering from civil war. It anchors each citizen to their birthplace, and that is the only place where they will be guaranteed to receive healthcare and education. Defenders of *hukou* assert that thanks to the system, belts of extreme poverty have not sprung up around major metropolitan areas, like in Brazil or India. But most Western and Chinese analysts agree that it is a profoundly unfair system that relegates internal migrants to second-class status. It is a highly polemic issue within the Chinese government.

13. According to an article published in the December 12, 2010, issue of *The People's Daily* (留守儿童人数近5800万 逾8成隔代或临时监护).

14. Data from China's official 2005 census.

15. According to China's National Office of Statistics, the median monthly salary earned by a *mingong* in 2010 was 1,600 yuan ($250), compared with the median salary of 2,687 yuan ($418) earned by Beijing-born workers.

7. China 2.0

1. According to Alexa.com and Google's DoublClick Ad Planner.
2. China Internet Network Information Center, September 2012.
3. 2008 study by TNS, a market research company.
4. China Investment Corporation, 2011.
5. China is the biggest market for the newest generation of smartphones, surpassing the US in 2011.
6. Chinese-American sociologist Tricia Wang sums up the phenomenon very well in her piece "Sleeping at Internet Cafes: The Next 300 Million Chinese Users," which can be found at www.triciawang.com.
7. The Chinese BBS sites began in the nineties. Among the most popular was the groundbreaking Shuimu Tsinghua, the most trusted by university students. The big corporations, associations and, of course, the government launched their own BBS forums. No one wanted to be left behind.
8. In 2012, 9.1 million students took the *gaokao*, competing for merely 6.85 million spots in Chinese universities. Since 2010, every year fewer students take the test, which many experts view as an effect of the one-child policy.
9. From reports by the news agency Xinhua and the newspaper *China Daily*, based on data from the Ministry of Education.
10. The most prestigious universities in China, equivalent to the Ivy League schools in the United States, are the University of Beijing, or Beida, an abbreviation of Beijing Daxue, for the humanities; Tsinghua University, for sciences; and the University of Fudan in Shanghai, renowned for its economics department.
11. The number of demonstrations or massive incidents, as civil unrest is officially called in China, in 2009, according to two studies conducted by the University of Nankai in 2011. However, unofficial sources like Sun Liping, a professor at Tsinghua University, estimate a larger number:

according to him, in 2010 China was rocked by 180,000 protests, riots and other mass incidents.

12. Chapter Two provides more details on this taboo episode, so critically important to contemporary Chinese history.

13. In March 2010, Google considered shutting down their site in China, if censorship of Web searches could not be stopped. They ultimately decided to redirect Chinese users visiting their site to Google Hong Kong, a semiautonomous Chinese territory, where they can access all the prohibited terms.

14. Some human rights organizations have charged that corporations including Cisco and Yahoo have provided information on activists and journalists to Chinese authorities. The companies maintain that they have no choice but to follow Chinese law, which requires them to give this information in order to maintain their business licenses.

15. One example is the blogger Guo Baofeng, arrested in July 2009 in the coastal city of Xiamen. He was twenty-five years old, and had sent a video to his followers on the Web of a mother accusing the local authorities of raping her daughter. Guo asked for help in Chinese and English on Twitter.

16. The initial round of treatment lasts between one and three months, but if the desired results are not obtained within that time, it is extended. When I visited the Tao Ran Center for Internet Addiction Treatment in Beijing, the first of its kind in China, in 2009, one teenager had already spent thirteen months there, and still had not been released.

17. According to the Chinese Academy of Social Sciences.

18. "We Need a Clear Definition of Pornography," by Zhang Cong. The article can be found at: http://www.china.org.cn/opinion/2010-01/18/content_19260104.htm.

19. These parodies have spawned an entire online counterculture called *egao* (恶搞), characterized by the satire of mainstream products, that could be loosely translated as "the evil work of humor."

20. In July 2009, in the autonomous region of Xinjiang in the west of China, violent clashes broke out between Muslim Uyghurs, who are the largest ethnic group, and Han Chinese migrants. According to official reports, 197 people died, and over 1,700 were injured. It was the bloodiest revolt China has experienced over the past two decades. Approximately 1,400 people were detained, and one of the first measures the government took

was to cut off the region's access to the Internet. Service was disrupted for ten months. In November 2010, the social networking site Fanfou was reactivated.

21. "From Red Guards to Cyber-Vigilantism to Where Next?" by Rebecca McKinnon, *R Conversation*, February 2009.
22. When I had this conversation with Ma Chengcheng, no concrete measures had yet been announced, but as of March 16, 2012, the Chinese government requires all Weibo users to provide real personal information including real names and identity numbers.
23. The US Army and the FBI keep far more personal data on file on its citizens than China. Google and Facebook, two American companies, are the largest proprietors of personal information in the world.

8. A Prostitute in Secret

1. "The East is Red" (东方红, Dongfang Hong) is the quintessential Chinese revolutionary song. The lyrics exalt former President Mao Zedong. During the Cultural Revolution (1966–1976) it was the Chinese National Anthem. It was broadcast over loudspeakers every morning and night in every town across the country. Today, for many Chinese the song is simply a part of their cultural heritage, not necessarily a tribute to Maoism.
2. The official retirement age for Chinese government employees is sixty for men, and fifty-five for women. Workers in state-run factories may retire at fifty.
3. Chongqing is one of the four municipalities with special status, which are dependent on China's central government.
4. The sixth generation of Chinese filmmakers includes directors like Jia Zhangke, Wang Xiaoshuai and Zhang Yang, who graduated from the Beijing Film Academy and the Central Institute of Drama in the late eighties and nineties. They broke artistically from their predecessors and crudely depicted China's social problems on the big screen through stories about rock bands, drifters with no future, apartments with no heat, and back-alley abortions. They have been compared with the Italian neorealists or cinema verité for their almost documentary-style storytelling.
5. In China prostitutes often call each other "sisters."

6. Sour prune juice or *suanmeitang* (酸梅汤) is a very typical drink in China. It is made of smoked black prunes and sugar.
7. Beijing has five major roads that circle the city, known as rings. They go from the second to the sixth, since there was never a first ring. The second ring surrounds the historic district, and the sixth is nine to twelve miles outside of the city center. The government is planning to build a seventh ring to alleviate traffic congestion.
8. UNAIDS 2012 *China AIDS Response Progress Report.*
9. Data from a 2006 study conducted by the People's University of Beijing's Institute of Research on Sexuality and Gender.
10. According to the NGO Human Trafficking, every year in China, organized crime rings abduct between ten and twenty thousand people. Nine out of ten victims are women and children forced into the sex trade, and/or are forced to work as slaves. And some women may be abducted and forced to marry some single man who has paid for them.
11. This is a pseudonym to protect her identity. "Meimei", as Wu calls her, means "little sister."
12. Wu and Zhen call each other respectively "big sister" and "little sister," like good friends do in China.

9. Beijing, Seen from a Taxi

1. Official data from March 2012.
2. According to Credit Suisse estimates in 2009, four of every ten city dwellers could afford a midpriced car if they qualified for financing, and nine of every ten residents of the countryside could manage to buy a low-priced economy car.
3. Only 2.9% of Chinese owned their own cars in 2009, one of the lowest rates of car ownership in the world, according to Credit Suisse, which estimates that in 2020, there will be 148 vehicles for every thousand Chinese citizens.
4. In Beijing the number of new registrations allowed was reduced from 740,000 to 240,000 per year.
5. Car sales fell by 6% in the first two months of 2012 compared with the same period of the previous year, according to the Chinese Association of Car Manufacturers.

6. *Urumqi* is the capital of the autonomous region of Xinjiang, in the far west of China, where most of the people are Muslim and ethnically Uyghur.

7. The Mongols conquered China in 1271, establishing their own dynasty, the Yuan, founded by Kublai Khan, and using Beijing as their capital.

8. A *siheyuan* (四合院) is a grouping of four buildings situated in a rectangle, leaving an open patio in the middle to provide light and ventilation.

9. Chapter ten discusses in more detail the problems inherent with urban development in China, and the forced expropriations of property.

10. Many of the wall's doors survive in Beijing's collective memory in the names of some neighborhoods, like Chongwenmen, Chaoyangmen, Dongzhimen and Xizhimen (the word *men* (门) means door).

11. For Mao, bringing down the wall was about politics. By 1970, it had been demolished almost in its entirety.

12. Zhang Xiaodong was referring to the fact that his friend's grandson would be born in the Year of the Dragon, which began in February 2012.

13. Data from the official *China Daily*, February, 2012.

14. The *dongbeiren* (东北人) or people from the northeast are those from the provinces of Liaoning, Jilin and Heilongjiang. The Chinese harbor many prejudices against their fellow countrymen, based on where they are from.

15. Mr. Lu was referring to the Chinese who are ethnically Uyghur, and Muslim, which are the majority in the Autonomous Region of Xinjiang. The Uyghurs suffer discrimination in the major cities like Beijing, especially since the uprising in their region in July 2009. See more on those events in the chapters "Kidnapped by His Own Government" and "The Dark Side of China."

16. The first group of Red Guards was formed at Tsinghua University in Beijing, in May 1966. On August 18 that year, Mao unleashed these radical students for the first time in Tiananmen Square. After that, the movement expanded throughout China.

17. The historical archives of the Cultural Revolution, declassified in 2009 and available to the public in the Municipal Archives of Beijing, describe how in the classrooms Maoist doctrine and revolutionary songs were reviewed for hours. They only spent a few minutes a day studying mathematics.

18. Mitter, Rana. *Modern China: A Very Short Introduction*, Oxford: Oxford University Press, 2008.

19. The "Down to the Countryside Movement (*shangshanxiaxiang yundong*, 上山下乡运动) forced hundreds of thousands of students in the cities to be sent to rural areas, in a kind of forced reeducation.

20. There is no official number of deaths. Estimates vary from hundreds of thousands to several million. Experts like Pulitzer Prize-winning journalist Ian Johnson leave the figure open.

21. Yi, Zheng, *Scarlet Memorial: Tales of Cannibalism in Modern China*. Boulder, Colorado: Westview Press, 1996.

22. Between 1966 and 1976, China's gross domestic product plunged by 40%.

23. That was the case for the Red Guards Jung Chang and Zhai Zhenghua, whose autobiography explains how he participated in the killings, convinced he was acting as a good revolutionary. Zhai Zhenhua, *Red Flower of China: An Autobiography*. New York: Soho, 1992.

24. Many books with testimony of former Red Guard soldiers had been published before, but never a report on how some were now asking their victims for forgiveness.

25. Mitter, Rana. *Modern China: A Very Short Introduction*. Oxford: Oxford University Press, 2008.

26. The term comes from one of the five most famous books of Confucius. Since 2002, it has become a standard part of the Government's rhetoric.

27. Increased internal consumption is a top priority to Chinese officials, especially since the Western economic crisis began in 2008 and product orders from China plummeted.

28. Data from China's Ministry of Health.

29. Chirping crickets are known as *guo guo* to differentiate them from the *qu qu*, which is used for fighting crickets, a popular pastime in China.

30. I met with Zhang Xiaodong before the North Korean dictator's death.

31. Chinese tourists have certain "privileges" in North Korea because their government is the closest thing to an ally that Pyongyang has. They can arrive by train and step a few feet closer to the highly militarized 38th parallel.

10. The Dark Side of China

1. At her request, I have given Linda a pseudonym and have not identified the television network.

2. The organization cites witness testimony in their report *Uprising in Tibet. March 10–April 30, 2008.*

3. The journalist James Miles of *The Economist* was the only reporter who was in Llasa, because when the protests broke out he was there on an official tour.

4. The German networks RTL and n-TV issued apologies. Others such as CNN and Der Spiegel issued statements denying accusations of manipulation, and defending their impartiality. CNN later apologized for the opinions expressed by commentator Jack Cafferty on Tibet, which had prompted a wave of criticism from China.

5. China is divided into 22 provinces (by Beijing's count there are 23, because they claim the island Taiwan as a province), five autonomous regions (associated with the largest ethnic minority groups, as in Tibet's case), four municipalities (large cities with a structure similar to that of the provinces) and two special administrative regions (Hong Kong and Macao).

6. Those clashes resulted in the deaths of tens of thousands of Tibetans. The Dalai Lama and approximately one hundred thousand followers fled Tibet on foot, crossing the Himalayas into India and Nepal.

7. The *fengqin* (愤青) are not a homogenous group, but share a strong sense of nationalism and an aggressive stance on international politics. They believe the Communist Party is too weak in its relationships with the U.S., Japan, Taiwan, Xinjiang and Tibet. Some justify certain actions Mao Zedong took during the Great Leap Forward and the Cultural Revolution.

8. There are no official figures. The international organization the Centre on Housing Rights and Evictions (COHRE) puts the number at 1.5 million, taking into account data from most sources that have investigated the subject. But on the Chinese government's official Web site China.org, the journalist David Ferguson disputes that figure, asserted that COHRE counted every single person that had moved in Beijing since 2000. His commentary, "Beijing's 1.5 Olympic Evictions: The Making of a Western Media Myth," is posted at: http://www.china.org.cn/china/2008-11/12/content_16752591.htm.

9. The struggle of the petitioners is discussed in greater detail in Chapter Two.

10. Data from the Chinese Academy of Social Sciences.

11. According to a study cited in the daily Nanfang Zhoumo.

12. Daniel Pearl, an American citizen, was *The Wall Street Journal*'s Southeast Asia Bureau Chief. In 2002 he traveled to Pakistan to research a story on Al-Qaeda. A month after he was kidnapped, his captors, an extremist Islamic group, released a video showing him being decapitated.

13. But soon, correspondents from Al Jazeera's English-language channel would be subjected to the same kind of harassment the other foreign networks experienced. Their relationship with government authorities went from bad to worse until in May 2012 the channel was forced to close its Beijing office because its correspondent had been expelled from the country. It was the first foreign reporter to be expelled in years.

14. Ranking on freedom of the press for 2011–2012, by Reporters Without Borders.

15. From a report by the Committee to Protect Journalists, December, 2011.

16. The sentence stated that the information in Tan's report "was irrelevant and not credible." Source: Marga Zambrana (EFE Agency), quoting Human Rights Watch, February 2010.

17. Both directives were issued in September 2011.

18. The blog can be found at: http://zhenlibu.wordpress.com.

19. The term "protests" (literally, massive incidents, 群体性事件) encompasses labor disputes, the demolition and relocation of homes, expropriation of rural lands, incidents of contamination, etc. According to experts at the Academy of Social Sciences, the number of these conflicts has increased notably in recent years.

20. The special can be found in Chinese at: http://magazine.caijing.com.cn/2010-10-24/110550933.html.